The Christmas Tree

Books by the Author

GARDEN FLOWERS IN COLOR

VEGETABLE GARDENING IN COLOR

ANNUALS FOR YOUR GARDEN

GARDEN BULBS IN COLOR (co-author)

LITTLE SAINTS OF CHRISTMAS

THE CHRISTMAS TREE

Christmas. the fete of the home and the heart, centers around the Christmas tree. Decorations
in the contemporary manner emphasize the form of this clipped cedar tree

The Christmas Tree

An EVERGREEN GARLAND Filled with
History, Folklore, Symbolism,
Traditions, Legends and Stories

DANIEL J. FOLEY

Color Photography
PAUL E. GENEREUX

Line Drawings
CHARLOTTE EDMANDS BOWDEN

CHILTON COMPANY · BOOK DIVISION
Publishers
PHILADELPHIA AND NEW YORK

Published in Philadelphia by Chilton Company,
and simultaneously in Toronto, Canada,
by Ambassador Books, Ltd.

CREDITS FOR COLOR PAGES: *Martin Luther's Christmas Tree* and
Christmas Tree at Strassburg by Pauline Baynes for *The Illustrated London News*, Christmas Number 1958. *Victorian Tree*,
courtesy Historical Society of Old Newbury. *Outdoor Tree*,
upper left, arranged by Mrs. R. Whitmore Teiner. *Doll Tree*,
upper right, courtesy Wenham Historical Association. *Topiary
Tree*, lower left, arranged by Mrs. Edward Woll. *Frosted Tree*,
lower right, exhibited by Hamilton-Wenham Garden Club.
Color photographs by Paul E. Genereux.

Library of Congress Catalog Card Number 60-16234

Designed by William E. Lickfield

Manufactured in the United States of America
by Quinn & Boden Company, Inc., Rahway, N. J.

Contents

To

GEORGE LAUMAN LAVERTY

In Appreciation

THE PLANNING AND WRITING of this book has been truly a labor of love. But it might never have been completed without the patience and help of countless friends and associates who have shared their enthusiasm, knowledge, and skill with me over a period of years.

To Dorothy Garfield for typing the manuscript and tending to countless details that have made my task pleasant and rewarding, I express my deep gratitude.

To Charlotte Edmands Bowden, who brought this story to life with nearly two hundred inimitable sketches, sparing neither time nor effort to lavish her talent.

To Paul E. Genereux who, over a period of six years, was ever ready to meet my requests for photographs in color and black-and-white. Except where indicated, all black-and-white photographs are from his files.

To Priscilla Sawyer Lord, who loaned me her great library of Christmas literature, as well as countless mementoes of Christmas. For numerous suggestions and advice, and for her carefully selected list, "Children's Books About the Christmas Tree," I am deeply grateful.

To Francis X. Weiser, S.J., Emanuel College, Boston, Massachusetts, author of *The Christmas Book, Handbook of Christian Feasts and Customs* and many other volumes, for sharing the fruits of his research in Germany and America; Dr. Alfred L. Shoemaker, Pennsylvania Folklore Society, Kutztown, Pennsylvania, for making available his exhaustive research on the Christmas Tree Lady of the Nation, for numerous items from her files, and J. Screiber, Wooster College, Wooster, Ohio, for use of his research material; Frances Dianne Robotti, New York City, author and researcher, for her personal interest and assistance; Mrs. Warder I. Higgins, Butte, Montana, The Christmas Tree Lady of the Nation, for numerous items from her files, and A. M. Sowder, Extension Forester of the U.S. Forest Service, for many items of information.

For assistance with various tasks relating to research, translating, illustration, and technical advice, my hearty thanks to: The Secretaries and Managers of Chambers of Commerce in the numerous communities throughout the country; Miss Lily Abbott; The Arrangers of Marblehead; Mrs. Julia Barrows; Mrs. Philip Batchelder; Brother Benignus; George A. Billias; Donald T. Bonnell; The Staff of the Boston Athenaeum; Dr. Harold Bow-

ditch; Mrs. John Bradford; Miss Margaret Brine; Mrs. Winthrop L. Carter; Charleston County Library; Charleston Library Society; Mrs. Harry Cobb; Mrs. Chester Cooke; Mrs. Charles H. P. Copeland; Corning Glass Works, Wellsboro, Pennsylvania; Francis C. Coulter; Martha B. Darbyshire; Brother Dennis Joseph; Robert A. Edwards; Robert L. Edwards; Emmanuel College Library; Mr. and Mrs. Ralph E. Ericson; The Staff of the Essex Institute Library; Dean A. Fales, Jr.; Miss Winnifred Foley; Miss Lauren Ford; Mrs. William W. K. Freeman; Rev. John M. Gessell; Mrs. Richard Hall; Mr. and Mrs. C. A. B. Halvorson, Jr.; Hamilton-Wenham Garden Club; Historical Society of Old Newbury; *Horticulture* Magazine, and Anne Hawkes Hutton. Also to Mrs. C. A. Haywood Hovey; Mr. and Mrs. L. P. Keeler; Dr. George L. Laverty; Mrs. Pierre Lounsbury; Miss C. Sally Low; Miss Katherine VanEtten Lyford; Francis J. Lynch; Lynn Public Library; Rev. Miles P. McKey; Mary Lane McMillan; Marie Lomas Main; Marblehead Public Library; Miss Margaret D. Mosimann; Pauline Bendl Murphy; Museum of Fine Arts, Boston; Mrs. Roy Nelson; Mrs. Jerome Ottmar; Mrs. Benjamin W. Partridge, Jr.; Mrs. Louis Phaneuf; Mrs. Cadis Phipps; Miss Genevieve Pinkos; Mrs. Charles A. Potter; Mrs. Robert G. Richards; Mrs. Edward Richardson; Mrs. William H. Riley; Amelia McSwiggin Rawding; Mrs. Gordon W. Roaf; Miss Virginia Rugheimer; Salem Athenaeum; The Staff of the Salem Public Library; Mrs. Frank Hayward Sawyer; Mrs. Elwood W. Schafer; A. M. Sowder; Mrs. James J. Strayer; Mrs. George E. Taylor; Sarah Wingate Taylor; Washington Cathedral; Mr. and Mrs. Maurice Weiner; Wenham Historical Society; Mrs. R. L. Wiggin; Mrs. Frances R. Williams, and Mrs. Edward Woll.

I am grateful to the following authors and publishers for permission to include the stories and legends in Chapter XIV.

The Stephen Daye Press for *The Miracle of the Fir Tree,* by Jean Variot, translated from the French by Leon King.

Houghton Mifflin Co. for *The Peterkins' Christmas Tree* reprinted from *Peterkin Papers,* by Lucretia P. Hale.

Horticulture Magazine and the author for "The Kissing Bunch Still Hangs High," by Katherine VanEtten Lyford.

Holt, Rinehart and Winston for *The Christmas Tree Ship* from *The Chicago,* copyright 1942, by Harry Hansen.

To *The Illustrated London News* for permission to use paintings by Pauline Baynes which appeared in the Christmas Supplement, 1958.

To the U.S. Forest Service and the Corning Glass Works for photographs, and to all the decorators of Christmas trees and makers of garlands who allowed me to photograph their handiwork. These illustrations are acknowledged individually as they appear.

Daniel J. Foley

Salem, Massachusetts

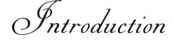

Introduction

A LITTLE EVERGREEN TREE or a big one ornamented with baubles and tinsel and gleaming with lights has come to be our symbol of Christmas. All over America and in nearly every country of Europe, extending even to Asia and the far-flung outposts of civilization, this colorful and decorative object has a very special kind of meaning. Not more than a century ago Charles Dickens was referring to the Christmas tree as "that pretty German toy." Even then it was not new, but its spread from Germany had been somewhat slow over a period of 250 years. Few of the royal family in England or the populace at large in the 1840's realized that here was the paradise tree in new dress revived from medieval miracle and mystery plays dating back to forgotten times. In America the Pennsylvania German settlers of the 19th century made it the center of their "home and heart fete" and, wherever they traveled and set up homes, men and women of German origin introduced their beloved symbol of Christmas with reverence, devotion, and joy. A truly novel idea, the decorated evergreen tree, proved to be a happy inspiration for the rediscovery of Christmas in the midst of hostile influences in America, a century ago.

This much-loved jewel of Christmas, with a background of folklore nearly as rich as that of the Christmas crib, radiates the sentiment and warmth of the Ageless Story. It has inspired scores of legends and an endless number of stories. Poets and composers have made it the subject of their praise and, for countless millions of children, it has been the acme of their hopes and the answer to their dreams. Likewise, for all of us who love Christmas and see its glory and its meaning through the eyes of children, the tree will be forever bright and sparkling.

Now each year at Christmas, forty million decorated evergreen trees brighten this land to herald the greatest of feast days and holidays in the modern world. Practically unknown a century ago, the Christmas tree has become so much an integral part of the season of greatest joy that we would not feel the presence of Christmas without the festive tree. How and when it came to us and how its popularity grew have been told in fact and fiction a thousand times, but most of the accounts, fanciful and delightful as they are, have overlooked its true origin.

Is it a pagan symbol, or was it inspired by a passage out of Isaiah? Or did it really come out of the Garden of Eden? To get a proper setting for the Tree and what it means, we must turn the pages of history and look into the very beginning of Christmas. The spirit imbued by Peace on Earth to Men of Good Will brought a new meaning and a new kind of hope to a weary world nearly 2000 years ago. That spirit, although dimmed at times by war and pestilence and the greed of men, has become, nonetheless, our Light of the World, symbolized in countless ways and most dramatically in the Christmas tree.

In an age dominated by science, with undue emphasis on things literal and factual, we tend to lose sight of another side of our nature—that which deals with myth and symbol. These inherent attributes are part of us more than we may often admit or realize. Like traditions, they explain in a simple, almost unbelievable way, things we accept and understand without knowing why.

Regardless of its size or form, whether live or artificial, highly ornamented with baubles, lights, and fancy ornaments or decked with homemade cookies, nuts and gum drops, it matters not—the Christmas tree, topped by a shining star reminiscent of Bethlehem, carries a precious message. From the oldest chronicler of the most ancient legend whose name has been lost in the mists of time, to the youngest schoolgirl who writes a prize story about the Christmas tree, this message remains fresh and universal.

The best stories about the Christmas tree have probably never been written and never may be put on paper, for much of the feeling imbued by a glistening evergreen, at this hallowed time of year, is difficult to put into words. It is a kind of co-mingling, or blending, if you will, of sentiment, awe, and wonder. To capture, or as it were, to recapture in cold type that warmth and mirth is not easy. Nor should it be. It is something we sense from within and it belongs happily in the realm of memories—not real perhaps—an image too bright and too colorful for our everyday world, for "it sings its own song without words in all our hearts."

CHAPTER I

Christmas Through the Ages

DOWN through the ages, men of every degree and rank, savage or civilized, have set apart certain days in different seasons of the year for performing ceremonials and enjoying themselves in a variety of ways. Thus we have holidays which were originally holy days, when men are able to rise above the humdrum of commonplace existence and shake off the fetters of monotonous routine that are a part of everyday living.

That versatile English essayist Gilbert Keith Chesterton, who always had something expressive and convincing to say about the good things in life, once posed the question, "Why do we have festivals and holidays?" In answering, he wrote, "We tend to tire of the most eternal splendors, and a mark on our calendar, or a crash of bells at midnight maybe, reminds us that we have only recently been created."

Holidays and festivals tend to stimulate our thoughts and arouse in us a new awareness of our spiritual duties coupled with the fact that there is joy in life which cannot be overlooked. In his fascinating book, *Christmas in Ritual and Tradition,* Clement A. Miles summed it up most warmly when he wrote: "It is difficult to be religious, impossible to be merry, at every moment of life, and festivals are as sunlit peaks, testifying, above dark valleys, to the eternal radiance."

The story of Christmas is best presented in two parts: that which deals with history and traditions of the birth of Christ as observed in the period which extends from Advent to Epiphany, and that which deals with those remnants of pagan traditions and customs predating the Christian era. These include the winter solstice, the Saturnalia, and all the attendant ceremonies delegated to that time of year which were observed from November through January.

It is customary with many people to confuse the two. Often, in their attempt to blend these widely diverse kinds of observance, they lose sight of the one and play up the other. Each has its place in history, and each is a part of our heritage. To enjoy and to live the Christmas season to the fullest, and to best understand Christmas, we need to see and understand the roots from which this season of seasons emerged.

Into a tired old world nearly two thousand years ago, came a ray of hope, a bright light. A Saviour was born. "And it came to pass in those days, that there went out a decree from Caesar Augustus, that all the world should be taxed. And this taxing was first made when Cyrenius was governor of Syria. And all went to be taxed, every one into his own city.

"And Joseph also went up from Galilee, out of the city of Nazareth, into Judea, unto the city of David, which is called Bethlehem; because he was of the house and lineage of David: To be taxed with Mary his espoused wife, being great with child. And so it was, that, while they were there, the days were accomplished that she should be delivered. And she brought forth her first-born son, and wrapped him in swaddling clothes, and laid him in a manger; because there was no room for them in the inn.

"And there were in the same country shepherds abiding in the field, keeping watch over their flock by night. And, lo, the angel of the Lord came upon them, and the glory of the Lord shone round about them: and they were sore afraid. And the angel said unto them, Fear not: for, behold, I bring you good tidings of great joy, which shall be to all people. For unto you is born this day in the city of David a Saviour, which is Christ the Lord. And this shall be a sign unto you; Ye shall find the babe wrapped in swaddling clothes, lying in a manger. And suddenly there was with the angel a multitude of the heavenly host praising God, and saying, Glory to God in the highest, and on earth peace, good will toward men.

"And it came to pass, as the angels were gone away from them into heaven, the shepherds said one to another, Let us now go even unto Bethlehem, and see this thing which is come to pass, which the Lord hath made known unto us. And they came with haste, and found Mary, and Joseph, and the babe lying in a manger. And when they had seen it, they made known abroad the saying which was told them concerning this child. And all they that heard it wondered at those things which were told them by the shepherds. But Mary kept all these things, and pondered them in her heart. And the shepherds returned, glorifying and praising God for all the things that they had heard and seen, as it was told unto them." (Luke 2: 1-20)

"Now when Jesus was born in Bethlehem of Judea in the days of Herod the king, behold, there came wise men from the east to Jerusalem, Saying, Where is he that is born King of the Jews? for we have seen his star in the east, and are come to worship him. When Herod the king had heard these things, he was troubled, and all Jerusalem with him. And when he had gathered all the chief priests and scribes of the people together, he demanded of them where Christ should be born. And they said unto him, In Bethlehem of Judea: for thus it is written by the prophet, And thou Bethlehem, in the land of Juda, art not the least among the princes of Juda: for out of thee shall come a Governor, that shall rule my people Israel.

"Then Herod, when he had privily called the wise men, enquired of them diligently what time the star appeared. And he sent them to Bethlehem, and said, Go and search diligently for the young child; and when ye have found him, bring me word again, that I may come and worship him also.

"When they had heard the king, they departed; and, lo, the star, which they saw in the east, went before them, till it came and stood over where the young child was. When they saw the star, they rejoiced with exceeding great joy. And when they were come into the house, they saw the young child with Mary his mother, and fell down, and worshipped him: and when they had opened their treasures, they presented unto him gifts; gold, and frankincense, and myrrh. And being warned of God in a dream that they should not return to Herod, they departed into their own country another way." (Matthew 2: 1-12)

"Then Herod, when he saw that he was mocked of the wise men, was exceeding wroth, and sent forth, and slew all the children that were in Bethlehem, and in all the coasts thereof, from two years old and under, according to the time which he had diligently enquired of the wise men. Then was fulfilled that which was spoken by Jeremy the prophet, saying, In Rama was there a voice heard, lamentation, and weeping, and great mourning, Rachel weeping for her children, and would not be comforted, because they are not." (Matthew 2: 16-18)

The fact that the accounts found in the Bible do not give a specific date as to the birth of Christ may lead some to wonder why we celebrate Christmas on this particular day. Actually, there was no specific record of the birth of the Christ Child. In looking back into those days, it is easy to understand why. The ruling powers among the Greeks and the Romans certainly had no time for the birth of a Saviour, nor did they want one. Any threat to their temporal power was a threat to their comfort and security, as witness the dominant rule of King Herod and his attempt to destroy the newborn male children of that time. The early Christians, hiding as they did to protect their newly adopted faith, had little opportunity to celebrate Christmas publicly, nor would it have been wise to observe it privately in their homes. Yet they could cherish the occasion in their hearts, and such they obviously did.

Francis X. Weiser in *The Christmas Book* states that about the year 320, "The Church in Rome definitely assigned December 25 for the celebration of the birth of Christ. For a while, many Eastern churches continued to keep other dates, but toward the end of the fourth century, the Roman custom became universal. The church did not, of course, rule that we know the precise date of Christ's birth, but merely assigned a certain day in order to unify the celebration of a religious feast of such importance. The fact that December 25 was chosen does not seem to rest so much on historical findings, as in the desire to replace the popular pagan celebration of the winter solstice by the festivities of a truly Christian holiday."

Thus the date of Christmas as we know it has been observed since the year 400 throughout the world, except by the communicants of the Greek Orthodox Church. They adhere to the Epiphany date thirteen days later, since they have never accepted the change made in the calendar by Pope Gregory XIII in 1582. He it was who corrected the old Julian calendar which had been established by Julius Caesar in the year 40 B.C. At that time, the calendar was ten days behind the actual astronomical time. As Father Weiser points out: "Pope Gregory not only eliminated these ten days but provided for future accuracy by a simple but ingenious arrangement of Leap Year. The Greek churches, which followed the old Julian calendar, are still thirteen days behind our date." Epiphany, often referred to as Little Christmas, commemorates the manifestation of Christ's glory.

Christmas is known by various names in various countries. In Latin, it is the Feast or Birthday of Our Lord. The English word Christmas, meaning the Mass of Christ, is as close to the Dutch equivalent of Kersmis as it is to any of the names by which this season is known. Xmas, an abbreviated form of Christmas in which X represents the Greek letter *X*, usually translated into English as "Ch," has come into common use in this era of short cuts. The German, *Weihnacht*, which means sacred night, is somewhat broad in its concept but is generally accepted to refer to *the* holy night. Both names, Christmas and *Weihnacht*, did not appear until the eleventh century when the faith was well established in both countries. Actually, the feast of Christmas was introduced in Germany some two hundred years earlier. St. Boniface had been there in the eighth century, having traveled from England to Christianize the Germans.

The term "Noel," from the French, means birthday, or it may derive from a word meaning news. In either case, the reference is to the birthday of Christ or to news of that momentous event. It has its counterpart in the feast day names of Provence, Italy, Spain, Portugal, and Wales. Likewise, the Greek name, as those used in the various Slavic countries, refers to the birth of Christ or God.

Yule is another term used for Christmas and is derived from the Scandinavian tongue. Like many ancient terms, its origin has been disputed. If the root is from Old German, it means turning wheel, referring to the rising of the sunwheel after the winter solstice. Or it may derive from an Anglo-Saxon word meaning feast and referring to the celebration of the solstice. In any event, as handed down to us, Yule as used today refers to the Feast of Christmas.

Since Christmas occurs between two great pagan festivals, it is only natural that down through the ages it should have taken on some of the aspects of each. The Saturnalia, extending from December 17 to December 24, was an age-old observance of tribute to the god Saturn, whose name means plenty or bounty. It was a time of rejoicing, hilarity and merrymaking. All work ceased, and children were released from school. Misunderstandings, even battles between tribes, ceased at this time of year. Plants and flowers were used to deck public gathering places and the exchange of presents was a common practice. Curiously enough, little clay dolls and other trinkets were sold at fairs. Obviously, the children were not overlooked. Of prime significance is the spirit of brotherhood that prevailed at this season of the pagan year. And this humanitarian touch was carried over into the Christian observance of Christmas. Thus we see the warm feeling of Dickens harking back to pre-Christian times.

Some of the spirit of warmheartedness and kindliness expressed at this time of year, when social barriers are dropped and expressions of good will are exchanged on all levels, comes down to us directly from the Saturnalia, but along the road it was chastened by the coming of the Christ Child and refined in its cruder aspects. Processions with lighted tapers and torches, the exchange of gifts, with particular emphasis on the children, and party giving that required dressing up in weird costumes is remembered today only by the paper hats we wear at parties.

In the midst of all this gaiety one day was set aside to pay tribute to the birth of the Unconquered Sun, and it occurred on what corresponds to Christmas as we know it. It was the greatest feast of the Mithraic religion, the state religion of the Roman Empire, and the competitor of budding Christianity.

Another feast that took place at this time of year was the Cleansing of the Temple, which occurred in the latter part of December. Its significance must not be overlooked, since the followers of Christ professed Judaism and the dedication of the temple was a custom they had long known.

In adapting much of the Saturnalia, the early fathers captured the spirit of the festival, which was rebirth, and transformed it to signify the coming of Christ. And so an ancient festival was given a new meaning.

In the cold North, the Teutons observed the winter solstice, calling it by a word we know as "Yule." Because the nights were long, it was referred to as the twelve nights. In early January came the Kalends, marking the beginning of a new year. It was a time for elections to public office, also for feasting and merriment. The comic note was personified in actors known as mummers, who dressed up in grotesque costumes made of animal skins and paraded through the streets. The spirit of the occasion was best exemplified in the wishes of happiness and prosperity that were exchanged, a custom which lingers on in our New Year's activities. In the writings of Libanius we find this vivid description:

"The festival of the Kalends is celebrated everywhere as far as the limits of the Roman Empire extend . . . The impulse to spend seizes everyone . . . People are not only generous themselves, but also towards their fellow-men. A stream of presents pours itself out on all sides . . . the Kalends festival banishes all that is connected with toil, and allows men to give themselves up to undisturbed enjoyment. From the minds of young people it removes two kinds of dread: the dread of the schoolmaster and the dread of the stern pedagogue . . . Another great quality of the festival is that it teaches men not to hold too fast to their money, but to part with it and let it pass into other hands."

On every side we find pagan customs and practices coloring the great feast that we know as Christmas. Sometimes the merrymaking was raucous and coarse and men of all ages and situations in life went to excesses, much to the displeasure of the early Christian leaders. Their opposition was aimed not so much at the simple practices themselves as at the superstitions and the spirit of abandon which accompanied these observances. Yet, many of these heathen customs, refined and stripped of their coarser elements, envelop our firesides with a kind of atmosphere that is quite acceptable to our philosophy and way of life, since they have long been divested of their original intent and purpose.

The story of Christmas is entwined in tradition, folklore, and fancy which are much more familiar than many of the historic facts connected with this most joyous of holidays. It is the Day of Days in the entire year which boasts more cherished customs than any other. All of these are associated with joy, happiness, and good will and revolve around the family hearth. Christmas belongs primarily to children and all the rest of the world can best enjoy it and live its spirit by viewing Christmas through the eyes of a child, because it is the birthday of the most extraordinary Child ever born.

In the beginning, it was purely a day of spiritual observance, without any of the fanfare and color which now attend it. There were neither carols nor bells, nor gaily decorated trees, nor elaborate spreads on the banquet table. "It was a feast of the senses and a feast of the soul. Bethlehem, bathed in supernal light, was the exclusive object of wonder."

With the passing of the centuries, men have been inclined to forget the true significance of Christmas, blinded by the glitter of tinsel, the brilliance of light, the feasting, and the gift-giving that have come to surround this holiday. Thus we cannot hear the angels sing or see the true beauty that surrounds and envelops the Nativity at Bethlehem.

As the early teachers of Christianity made their way from country to country spreading the gospel of Christ, the Christmas observance became known in the old world. By the twelfth century all the nations of Europe

were familiar with Christianity and Christmas was celebrated with true devotion and joy. During this period many of our oldest carols, the Christmas plays, and dozens of colorful customs were developed and expanded from a Christian point of view. Traditions and legends began to grow in a period when the faith was very close to the populace at large. Myriads of little stories related with simple naïveté, all wondrous and filled with the glory of the Christ Child, were told and retold, often greatly embellished by each narrator.

The lighting of candles on Christmas eve and throughout the twelve days following, the burning of the Yule log, decorating with greens, elaborate preparations of food, and other festive practices were commingled with the devotions of Advent—the four weeks preceding Christmas. Little was overlooked in making ready for the feast that commemorated the arrival of the Light of the World. Many of the customs which have become part of Christmas had been observed in the preceding centuries. Some, known in pagan times, were adapted to the new philosophy of hope and love and their stories will unfold in the chapters that follow. But the old meanings had been transformed in the minds and hearts of the people. The rejoicing came to glorify the Christ Child, the life spring of salvation for mankind.

In the midst of all this joy came a great new source of light, bathed in the very spirit of the Child himself, who had already cast His radiance and image all across the world. Saint Francis of Assisi, from a humble hut in his beloved Umbrian hills, re-enacted the birth of Christ with such tenderness, beauty, and simplicity that it lives undimmed even in our chaotic age. On that eventful Christmas Eve in the year 1223, St. Francis brought to those assembled a warm and heartening and truly human concept of the manger at Bethlehem. He introduced a live ox and a donkey into his manger setting and the people of the village participated in re-enacting the event that had taken place some twelve hundred years earlier on that holy night. Nesta de Robeck records it all delightfully in her little book, *Saint Francis—The Herald of the Great King:*

"For Francis Christmas had always been the 'feast of feasts,' the feast of light and hope, of peace and joy and brotherly love, the day when 'Heaven and earth are made one,' when God 'condescended to be fed by human love.' He would have liked to see every poor man handsomely entertained, and every ox and ass be treated to double rations, and corn scattered for the birds.

"Giovanni willingly fell in with Francis's plan and arranged a manger filled with hay, and sent an invitation to all the friars and people of the neighborhood; 'and many brothers and good people came to Greccio during that night when the weather also was most beautiful. A great quantity of lights had been kindled, many songs and hymns were sung with great solemnity by

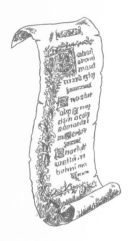

the many brothers, so that all the wood echoed with the sound, and the man of God stood before the manger filled with the utmost joy, and shedding tears of devotion and compassion.' "

Jacopone da Todi, to whom we attribute many of the most beautiful of our early carols, was born shortly after the death of Francis. He wrote with that same simple, direct approach, describing the creature comforts and all the little natural touches that made the Christ Child the loveliest of babes, a warm, cuddly person, sparkling with humanity and just as real as any of the little cherubs that were born to the folk who listened to his carols. For him "God made a little thing" and the Christ Child was "our sweet little brother." Here in simple language is a painting in words of the Madonna and her Child attributed to Jacopone, or to one of his followers, which expresses the very essence of the new spirit.

Come and look upon her child
Nestling in the hay!
See his fair arms opened wide,
On her lap to play!
And she tucks him by her side,
Cloaks him as she may!
Gives her paps unto his mouth,
Where his lips are laid.

She with left hand cradling
Rocked and hushed her boy,
And with holy lullabies
Quieted her toy . . .
Little angels all around
Danced, and carols flung;
Making verselets sweet and true,
Still of love they sung.

The significance of the crib was by no means unfamiliar to the world of that day. Records and relics dating back to the fourth century indicate this fact, and St. Francis and Jacopone brought it all to life.

In the thirteenth century the church was moved by a great change, a change that was to do much to humanize the emotional expression of religion and the truths of the faith. As Michael Harrison had expressed it: "There was a renaissance of the heart, rather than the mind."

The laity were able to participate more actively in the liturgy of the church, and in doing so they humanized it. Theology was reduced to its simplest terms, so that the unlettered folk (for most of the peasants had little learning) were able to comprehend the great mysteries of the life of Christ. It is a curious thing that the two men who brought about this great change in feeling, or sentiment, were St. Francis, the son of a wealthy silk merchant, and Jacopone da Todi, an aristocrat who had chosen to take on a new life as a working man, a peasant, and identify himself with the common people. As a result, his new understanding enabled him to write superbly, in a most charming, poetic form, and his poems, or songs, for they are truly musical and beautiful, have made us all feel the humanity of the birth of the Christ Child. For centuries these tender forms of expression have been the sum and substance of our most meaningful Christmas carols.

Holly and blue spruce make an attractive setting for the Holy Family. Arranged by Mrs. Frank Lenherr

Michael Harrison describes the new concept of the Baby Jesus, "As a loving little chap, as astonished as any peasant boy would be to find that he could perform miracles. This Christ-child uses, as we may understand, his magic but simple pleasures—even for childish revenges. It is because he is so simple, so peasant, so earthy, the Christ of the Medieval clod lives. Francis offered Him to the people, and the people, in one blinding flash of intuition, recognized Him as one of themselves and took Him—bib and nappie and all—into their homes and their hearts, and for His praise they told His story in verses as rude and simple and innocent as themselves: verses which, like their divine subject, will live forever."

Thus, the introduction of the Christmas carol, the popularization of the crib, and the rise of a whole imaginary world of legend and tradition, woven together, make a rich tapestry against which the Christmas observance from the twelfth to the sixteenth century flowered in all its beauty and glory.

At the same time, with so much spontaneous expression and the growth of the Miracle and Mystery plays which come in for more attention later in these pages, we find the rise of other observances, some of which were obviously colored by pagan influence. The demonstrations of the mummers, the grotesque costumes used for Christmas observances, the wild enthusiasm, the uncontrolled expressions of joy often took on a rather objectionable aspect. These excesses, although they were banned by the church, nonetheless persisted to the time when Christmas was banned as an observance, particularly in England.

The objections to Christmas by the Puritans, and their vigorous attempt to subdue the holiday, or rather, the whole series of days which had grown into an elaborate festal season, were not too effective. For there was ingrained in the hearts of the people a love for Christmas which no law or'rule could subdue.

It is curious to observe that this condition, despite the Reformation, did not exist in Germany, and many of the tenderest expressions of the Christmas observance were kept alive there by the Lutherans through the eighteenth century. It is from this warmhearted source that many of the traditions brought to America were rekindled and revived.

The spirit which made England merry died out with the suppression of Christmas; the new point of view was not so much colored by spontaneous devotion, or rather, by a deeply religious feeling as it was by a new kind of humanitarianism. The old devotional songs, or carols, were supplanted by popular ones relating to the feasting and drinking and ceremonials of the people that reflected another kind of Christmas. The humanitarianism of Dickens in the nineteenth century best exemplifies the whole change.

We often hear the old expression, "God rest you merry gentlemen," but in its original form it read, "God rest you merry, gentlemen," which translated into contemporary English means, "God rest you peacefully, gentlemen." This point is significant since it reflects the change in the whole spirit of Christmas as it was known then and as it exists, to a great extent, today.

CHAPTER II

Evergreen Symbols

THE USE of evergreens, cones, and fragrant herbs in the making of wreaths and garlands for festive occasions, and particularly for Christmas, is an ancient art dating back to the Egyptians a thousand years or more before the time of Christ. References to wreaths and garlands of leaves, flowers, and fruit can also be found in Oriental literature, in the traditions of the Persians, the ancient records of the Hebrews, and the rituals of the Druids. This practice among men is obviously a kind of universal expression of joy mingled with devotion, and can hardly be described as either a pagan or a Christian custom. Living plants exemplifying the essence of beauty helped to dispel the gloom of winter, and the evergreens particularly symbolized eternal life.

Certain flowers and plants symbolized honor, victory, achievement and were equally cherished for use on festive tables at holidays. An inherent love for the flowers and fruits of field and garden is more deeply rooted in the heart of man than is generally realized.

From the Persians the ancient Hebrews acquired their taste for floral *décor* and the Greek warriors brought these customs home from battle to their great cities. The Romans, captivated by the color and fragrance of the garlands they could fashion, used them to embellish their ceremonials. Small wonder then that a temple was erected to the goddess Flora some two hundred years before the time of Christ.

Although the decorative use of flowers and fruits continued to play a vital part in the everyday lives of the Greeks and Romans during the early centuries of the Christian era, the church fathers finally decreed that this pagan practice must cease. However, it was not long before the churchmen realized how meaningful and symbolic these deeply rooted traditions were and the ban was lifted. Early in the seventh century, St. Augustine of Canterbury was advised by the Pope not only to permit but to encourage such popular customs which were an inherent part of man's mode of self-expression.

Flowers and plants formerly associated with pagan deities were ascribed to the Madonna and the early Christian martyrs. Hepworth Dixon, noted English authority on plant lore, expressed the significance of the new concept

in these words: "The poetry no less than the piety of Europe ascribed to her (the Virgin Mary) the whole bloom and coloring of the fields and hedges." Consequently, the revival of interest in decking halls and churches on festive occasions and feast days reached a high pitch among peasants and nobles alike. Holly and ivy, evergreens, fragrant herbs, mistletoe, and other favorites were used lavishly for adornment to commemorate the long Yuletide holidays.

Holly, both the tree itself and its brightly berried branches, holds special significance for use at Christmas. The very name is believed to be derived from the word holy—thus holly tree from holy tree. Popular names long current in English folklore are Christmas, Christmas tree, and Prickley Christmas. It had been widely used in ceremonials long before the Christian era. The Druids considered holly sacred and used it in healing the sick. It would repel evil spirits and protect a house from lightning. Branches hung around the house and stable were a good omen, and it was believed that cattle would thrive if holly were placed where it could be seen on Christmas Day.

In parts of England and Germany hollies are referred to as "he" and "she," those with heavily spined leaves are known as the "he" hollies, while the smooth-leafed kinds are associated with the gentler sex. The types brought in for Christmas would determine, according to an old custom, who was to be head of the household for the coming year. The Scotch-Irish who settled Pennsylvania cherished this custom for many years and added to it the belief that if the holly were brought indoors in fair weather, the wife would rule the household, whereas if it were cut and brought in during a storm, then the man would be master for the coming year.

The lore connected with holly is rich indeed and the superstitions most extraordinary. It was believed to be unlucky if holly were left up after New Year's or Twelfth Night, hence the burning of the greens. In this case it was feared that spirits or ghosts might disturb the maidens of the household. Another old custom was that the holly had to be taken down before Shrove Tuesday. There were customs regarding the burning of holly. Some believed that it should never be thrown away, but burned, lest ill luck should affect those of the household; whereas in other places it was felt that it should be kept until the following year to protect the house from lightning.

Holly has been popular as a Christmas symbol all over the world. In Italy sprigs of this evergreen shrub are used in decorating the mangers at Christmas. In Germany it is known as *Christ dorn,* the thorn woven into the crown of the Crucifixion, and an old legend relates that before the berries were red they were yellow, and the wounds of Christ stained them red. Among the Pennsylvania Germans the holly berries represented the blood of Christ that issued from His wounds, and the white flowers of the tree were considered symbolic of the purity in which He was conceived.

Della Robbia swag using nuts, cones, artificial fruits. New England Farm and Garden Association

Artificial grapes, nuts and cones inspired by 15th-century decor. New England Farm and Garden Association

Taking her inspiration from the carving of Grinling Gibbons, Mrs. Myron B. Barstow created this classic ellipse with dried pods and cones, a permanent Christmas decoration

Traditional decorations add to the old world charm of the Beacon Hill residence of Mr. and Mrs. Charles Townsend. Doorways like this one made Charles Dickens feel at home in Boston

Among the first plants sighted by the Pilgrims who settled in Plymouth in 1620 was the native American holly, which was found then in great abundance all along the south shore of Massachusetts. As H. W. Dengler states in *The History of Holly in Murals,* it is not difficult to conjure up in our minds the emotions of the early settlers "on finding their first holly and of the speed at which they hastened to their wives to show them this cheerful reminder of their homeland. One especially conjectures on the sentiments and feelings of the Pilgrim women and girls at this first sight of the holly, for to womanhood, the old ties, the old superstitions, the old loves, and the old traditions are always the strongest. This way it has always been; this way it is always to be."

Ivy, an important plant in Greek mythology, was associated with Bacchus, the god of wine, and its associations with the beverage are numerous. Is was believed that the berries, taken before wine, would prevent intoxication. For ceremonials, garlands of ivy leaves were sometimes used to crown the poets. It was considered a symbol of love, because of its clinging habit of growth. Particularly in the Middle Ages it was held in high esteem for decorating, so much so that ivy was the subject of more than one Christmas carol.

Mistletoe, actually a parasitic plant found growing on trees, is steeped in ancient tradition and lore. Scandinavian mythology relates how the plant must always be suspended in order to serve as an instrument for good, since its earlier use had been one of destruction. Thus, when hung from the ceiling, members of the opposite sexes passing under it give one another a kiss of peace and love. With the Druids, this plant was especially sacred if found on an oak and cut with great ceremony, and it was used as a cure-all for many ills. As a decoration for homes, it was always hung, and together with holly and other greens provided shelter for the sylvan spirits in winter. For centuries, in many parts of Europe remnants of these ancient beliefs have lived on and the peasants cherished the occasions when they gathered the mistletoe. It is referred to as "bringing home Christmas," that pleasant pastime of gathering greens, cones, and berries for holiday decoration.

Boxwood, which was used by the ancient Hebrews in the Feast of the Tabernacles, is mentioned by the prophet Isaiah in describing the glory of the latter days of the church. "The glory of Lebanon shall come unto thee, the Fir-tree, the Pine-tree, and the Box-tree together, to beautify the place of my sanctuary." The poet Herrick tells us that box was used to replace the Christmas greens which were removed on Candelmas. Boxwood was kept up until Easter eve and then replaced with branches of the yew tree.

The delicately fragrant rosemary, with its needlelike leaves, silvery on one side, which remain evergreen in the warm parts of Europe, has long been used in Christmas decorations. The flowers of this shrub were once white, but

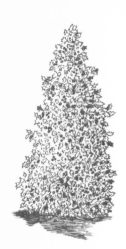

were changed to pale blue when the Virgin Mary spread her Infant's clothes on a rosemary bush to dry during the flight into Egypt. Rosemary brings happiness to those who use it, perfuming their houses on Christmas night. "A comforter of the brain," it is the herb sacred to remembrance, and there is an old notion that it makes the old young again. This herb of the sun was a prime favorite of St. Thomas More and in his time it was served up as a garnish with the boar's head at the Christmas feast.

To us in America laurel is somewhat different from the fragrant sweet bay of Europe, although the foliage is similar. We know it best as a source of flavoring in cookery. To the Greeks and Romans it was a sacred plant used to decorate statues of their gods, victorious athletes, poets, and renowned people. It served as a most appropriate cover for Caesar's bald head. The stories recounting its uses, its significance and its associations are truly fascinating, and because of these it has been widely used for decorating at Christmas. Yew, juniper, pine, and other greens, together with the fruits of roses, a wide variety of berries and cones from evergreens—all had a place in the decorating of homes and churches for the most significant of festal tides. Flowers, too, particularly the Christmas rose, the paper-white narcissus, the cyclamen, dwarf orange and lemon trees, the carnation, the poinsettia, heather, and a host of other colorful blooms have further enhanced the decorative schemes used at Christmas.

The worship of trees has had prime significance in the history of mankind down through the ages and extends back to those remote times when the world was made up of wandering tribes. Back in the misty days of the primeval forest, it was the business of new immigrants to found a central settlement known as a "mother town." When they cleared land, they always left a group of trees in the center of the clearing. Among the trees stood a central tree known as a "mother tree." From this source stemmed all action of life and pursuit of religious belief. As the settlements grew and additional communities were formed, those who went forth as pioneers took with them their household gods, their tribal ways of measuring time, and their customs. In the new settlement they lighted their first fires at the same times as their fathers had lit theirs and thus remained "chips off the old block."

From this ancient realm of tree worship associated with seasonal changes emerged the Christmas observance of the Yule log. In France it was known as *La Tronche*, the tree trunk, and was lighted for a few minutes on Christmas Eve. Then the fire was put out and the log covered with cloth. The children who came to observe were urged to beat the cloth with sticks to see if they could bring the log to life again, but always the effort was hopeless. They were then told to go aside and beg pardon for their faults, which had prevented Mother (that is, the tree) from being good to them. While the children were asking pardon for their faults, the parents assembled the presents that were to be given to them and hid them under the cloth. Then the children returned, again beat the cloth, and found the presents.

This custom may have originated in the Greek ceremony depicting the birth of Apollo and Artemis on the Xanthus River in Lycia and the Isle of Delos. The notion stems from the old tradition of the Mother Leto wor-

The holly cart

shipped under the form of a tree trunk or log, that is, from the mother tree of early village peoples.

The Yule log was considered the fire mother of the Sun God. Half burned on Christmas Eve after the gift ceremony, it was then stored as a protection against lightning. The ashes of the log were buried at the base of the roots of fruit trees to insure greater productivity in the coming year.

In that era of history which belongs to mythology, trees were believed to be spirits or to places where spirits could find shelter and protection. Eventually, trees took on the form of deities who were the guardians of fertility. Thus the legends and the lore of many countries led to a curious kind of tree worship with strong emphasis on their preservation and care.

The customs, beliefs, and ceremonies associated with growing trees of various kinds make fascinating reading, particularly when we approach these tales with an understanding of the reverence in which these living symbols were held.

Some of the curious practices of ancient times have persisted among the country folk of Europe even to this day. The ceremony of wassailing the fruit

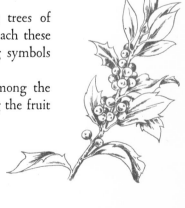

Burning
Bush

trees on Christmas Eve or morning was observed, to insure a good crop of fruit. It is an old nature symbol which makes us realize how close were the ties to the soil of the peasants who tilled it. Children's story books published in America even at the turn of this century gave fanciful accounts with pictures of this old custom.

Many of our familiar trees are closely associated with the Christmas tradition. The poplar, the cherry, the ash, the apricot, the apple, the hawthorn are rich in legends drawn from the folklore of every country in the old world. There is an old belief among the gypsies that the ash tree or twigs from it should be used to make the fire on Christmas Eve. They cherish the notion that this tree supplied the wood that made the fire that warmed Mary and Joseph and the Child Jesus on that first Christmas night in the cold cave at Bethlehem.

All the gala ceremony attendant on Maypole festivities is another manifestation of these ancient practices which have changed so much that today little remains of the age-old traditions. The crowning of a May Queen is tame indeed in comparison with the high jinks that surrounded this welcome to May in Shakespeare's time or even in the early nineteenth century. The pole, originally a tree, was brought into the village and set up in a prominent place. Dressed with garlands of leaves and flowers, it took on the appearance of a living tree. Dancing and merrymaking were the order of the day. The Maypole customs belong to the realm of nature lore and have become the basis for several flower festivals connected with Pentecost in conjunction with church ceremonies.

The Christmas tree as we know it today is often linked in the popular mind with these manifestations and beliefs. In our eagerness to assimilate all these notions, we tend to link them without being aware that the various customs stemmed from a wide variety of practices. All have a common source, but they developed and expanded as more emphasis was placed on a particular belief.

In Rome before Christianity took root, the ancient fig tree which had originally flourished on the banks of the Tiber was finally transported to the Comitium of the Forum, where it was widely known and revered. It was a slip of the tree beneath which the she-wolf had nursed Romulus and Remus who founded that ancient seat of civilization. Its care, preservation, and perpetuation make a most enchanting story full of marvels and wonders.

The Burning Bush mentioned in the Old Testament (Exodus 3:2, and Acts 7:30) served as a symbol of the Nativity and also of the Virgin Mary. It became a decorative motif in the catacombs as early as the third century and later appears in various expressions of religious art ranging from stained glass windows to the printed page. The root of Jesse became a vivid symbol

Jesse Tree

with the church fathers. St. Ambrose tells us: "The root is the family of the Jews, the stem Mary, the flower of Mary is Christ."

The similarities between the plant world and the animal realm were very real to men in early times. The resemblances between trees and plants displayed in their appearance in the various seasons and at different times of day made men aware of the mysterious power or forces of nature. Seasonal changes left a deep impression, inspiring an attitude of reverence and awe. Indeed, the many-sided concepts about trees and vegetation are easy to understand when we consider these facts.

Adam and
Eve Tree

Thus, the importance of trees as the source of human life and as the very beginning of the world falls into place. So, too, do the powers of good and evil, associated with plants. This universal instinct manifested itself in the Norse world tree, the Ash Yggdrasill which rose out of the ocean and supported the earth. The Hindus also had a world tree similar in qualities and virtues to the tree of Paradise, and so too did the Buddhists, the Iranians, and the Assyrians. Then there was the Mother tree of the Greeks, the Romans, and the Teutons, and the Chinese had their sacred willow.

The trees in the garden of Paradise were many in number but two stand out in religion, history, and literature. They are the Tree of Life and the Tree of Knowledge of Good and Evil. "And out of the ground made the Lord God to grow every tree that is pleasant to the sight, and good for food; the tree of life also in the midst of the garden, and the tree of knowledge of good and evil." (Genesis 2:9). The Tree of Life symbolized the source of sustenance for man to meet his physical and spiritual needs so long as he remained obedient. On the other hand, the fruit-bearing Tree of Knowledge of Good and Evil was a symbol to determine the worth of Adam and Eve.

The Tree of Life in Christian symbolism is exemplified in the Cross and its appearance in the Garden of Eden, as pictured to us both in the words of holy scripture and in old prints and paintings, may be described or defined as a prefiguration of it. What kind of tree it was has been discussed by scientists and theologians for centuries. It may have been a date palm, a banana, a fig, or a mountain ash. Its physical aspect and the species or kind is of little importance. Essentially it is a symbol, a very ancient one when we consider how deeply rooted is the tradition of trees in the life of man.

The Tree of Knowledge of Good and Evil is traditionally referred to as an apple tree, or more correctly as an apricot. Some claim it was actually a fig tree since Adam and Eve used fig leaves to clothe themselves after eating of the forbidden fruit. Others mention it as a palm, a citron, or a pomegranate. Pursuing this tradition further, we learn from several accounts of the origin of the Tree of Adam which eventually produced the wood for the Cross, the Symbol of Symbols in the Christian World.

Children in the Gay Nineties learned about the Yule log from prints in the pages of *Chatterbox*, a popular holiday annual for young people for more than forty years

CHAPTER III

Golden Legends

THE TRADITIONS surrounding the birth of Christ are as rich in their imagery as they are numerous and varied. On that eventful night, extraordinary occurrences took place. The animals expressed their joy by conversing and kneeling in homage to the Saviour. The birds came out of hibernation to sing of their great joy, and the bees stirred in their hives. The water in the rivers turned to wine. Most wonderful of all, the trees burst into bloom, despite the cold season of the year. All nature came alive and the world around Bethlehem shone with a brightness that exceeded moonlight, starlight, and sunlight. From this inspired legend many explanations, also legendary, arose, among them several to explain the existence of the Christmas tree.

This story, which had its origin in the writings of an Arabian geographer of the tenth century, became the accepted belief of folk throughout France, Spain, Germany, and Great Britain. In the life of St. Hadwigis, who lived about the end of the twelfth century, there appears this curious account: "Once, when she was young, on Christmas day somebody entered the room, saying, while she was sitting at the table, that a cherry tree in the garden stood in full blossom. She, on hearing this, sent him back in order to see whether the buds sprang from the lower or the upper part of the tree. He went, and on his return reported that the tree blossomed at its lower branches. But she said: 'That is a sign of the coming mortality. Many poor will die this year.' And as she foretold, so it happened."

The cherry is of special significance in this legend, for the tradition on which the cherry tree carol is based was long cherished in the popular mind. As the story goes, Joseph and Mary were walking together "in a garden gay, where cherries were growing on every spray." When Mary asked for some of the ripe fruit, Joseph refused, for he remembered the message of the angel, but the branches bent low so that Mary might pick:

And she shall gather cherries
By one, by two, by three.
"Now you can see, Joseph,
Those cherries were for me."

"O! eat your cherries, Mary,
O! eat your cherries now.
O! eat your cherries, Mary,
That grow upon the bough."

Joseph was humble indeed in asking pardon of Mary for his undue concern, for an angel appeared to her announcing that the King of the World would soon be born. Thus the cherry was dedicated to Mary and many medieval and renaissance painters have used the cherry in clusters, or in a bowl or basket, in rendering portraits of the Virgin Mary. There is a delightful old mystery play in which one of the shepherds presents the Christ Child with a bob of cherries. And tradition has it that Christ gave Saint Peter a cherry, reminding him at the same time not to despise little things.

It is generally believed that the legend of the Arabian geographer, together with the story of the cherry tree carol, made popular the custom of forcing small cherry trees in tubs for Christmas bloom. This was a type of Christmas tree, and some historians believe that it contributed greatly to the development of the Christmas tree as we know it today. The apricot also was used for this purpose. Albrecht Adam, noted German painter of the late eighteenth century, described one at his home in Nordlingen that stood in the corner of the room and was in full bloom at Christmas, reaching almost to the ceiling. These flowering trees were not only desirable ornamentally, but so keen was the enthusiasm for them that families vied with one another to see who could force the finest tree.

In like manner, branches of cherry, apricot, hawthorn, elder, lime, and horse chestnut were forced for Christmas by placing the branches in water. Both city dwellers and peasants enjoyed this custom. The flowering branches served as an oracle at this cold time of year when forced for the New Year. If the blooms on the forced stems were full and perfect, the omen was a good one, but if they were sparse or imperfect or failed to develop, the sign implied bad times. This custom took on many kinds of symbolic meaning according to the country in which it was practiced. The use of brightly colored flowers made of paper and cloth to decorate evergreen trees (first mentioned in 1605) could well stem from this custom of forcing flowering branches.

Accounts of apple trees bursting into bloom and in some cases producing fruit are attributed to the early fifteenth century. These tales were told for several centuries to follow and became an accepted part of the Christmas tradition in Germany. The folk at Nuremberg used to make pilgrimages to view a miraculous tree that "bore apples the size of a thumb" on the night of Christ's birth. However, these traditions are not as widely known as the story of the Glastonbury thorn.

This extraordinary tree is a variety of the common hawthorn. In the mild climate of Great Britain it flowers in late fall and early winter. This particular plant at Glastonbury became famous because for many years it blossomed religiously on Christmas Day and became known as the holy thorn.

As its fame spread, cuttings were taken and grafts were made from the original tree in order to perpetuate it. Before Christmas, it was customary for the villagers to take the branches indoors to force them for the holidays.

There are also accounts of walnuts and oaks that brought forth leaves at Christmas. So deeply entrenched were the associations of this wonderful tree that the Christmas following the official change of the calendar in September, 1752, became one of prime significance for the people of Glastonbury. In that year, September 2 was legally changed to September 14, making Christmas fall twelve days earlier than the previous year. This change caused a great stir among the local residents who were eager to discover how the holy thorn would perform.

At Quainton in Buckinghamshire two thousand people gathered on Christmas Eve carrying lanterns and candles to view a scion of the original Glastonbury Thorn. But there were neither buds nor blossoms to be found, so it was agreed by all assembled that the new style Christmas was not the true Christmas Day. In fact, many refused to observe that date set by the new calendar and would not attend church. At nearby Glastonbury, the thorn bloomed as usual on Christmas old style (January 5).

Within the last two hundred years this story has been recounted many times and has special significance for our day, since a scion of the famous white flowering thorn planted at the National Cathedral on Mount St. Albans in our nation's Capital has been closely observed since it was first set out. The late Very Rev. G. C. F. Bratenahl, Dean of the National Cathedral, became greatly interested in this legend and pursued the golden thread of the story with true scholarship. As a result, we have one of the most unusual and beautiful stories of this hallowed season.

After the Resurrection, the Christian leaders were sorely persecuted. Tradition has it that Joseph of Arimathaea, together with Mary and Martha, their brother Lazarus, and other disciples, escaped in a boat without sails or oars and were blown across the sea to Marseille in Southern France. Mary, Martha, and some of their companions remained there. With twelve companions, Joseph re-embarked in the little boat which carried them to Britain. They "proceeded inland after a time, and being wearied, they rested on a hill, now known as Weary-All-Hill, near Glastonbury. This occurred on Christmas Day. Here Joseph of Arimathaea plunged his staff into the ground, where it immediately took root, budded and blossomed. Every year since then at Christmas time it has bloomed, becoming known as the Holy Thorn of Glastonbury.

"The miraculous budding of Joseph of Arimathaea's staff was accepted as a token that the travelers had reached their journey's end. The King of the Country, Avigarus by name, received them kindly and gave them twelve

'Hides' of land (about 1400 acres) in Inis Witrin, a marshy tract afterwards called the Isle of Avalon. St. Joseph and his companions are said to have erected here a wattled church and wattled huts for themselves, establishing the first Christian mission in the British Isles."

Dean Bratenahl, fascinated by this legend, devoted considerable time and effort in tracing its history. Aware of the fact that behind many of our cherished traditions there is often a shred of truth, he pieced together old records and documents. Turning to a series of annals on church history prepared by Cardinal Boronius, sixteenth century librarian at the Vatican, he learned that Joseph of Arimathaea had sailed from Palestine in 41 A.D. Excavations made at Glastonbury at the turn if this century showed evidence of a village of structures made of wattles and other significant relics.

"What more natural," asks Dean Bratenahl, "than that Joseph of Arimathaea, a rich man, presumably with friends among the wealthy merchants of Tyre, should find asylum amongst them, after the martyrdom of St. Stephen?" It is well know that for almost a century B.C. the Carthaginian city and the merchants of Marseille, across the Mediterranean, were rivals in competition for the output of the tin mines of Britain. "What more logical," Dean Bratenahl again asks, "than that Joseph of Arimathaea should continue his journey along the sea routes these traders had followed, perhaps with their recommendations for hospitality at the hands of the Britons, until he reached the realm of King Avigarus, who received him hospitably, as recounted in the legendary version."

Christianity is known to have existed in some form in the British Isles during the first three centuries A.D. "How did it get there?" Dean Bratenahl poses the question, answering it by the exposition: ". . . among all the manifold explanations of the origin of Christianity among the Britons, nothing appears to touch the imagination as this story of Joseph of Arimathaea . . . ."

For centuries the Glastonbury Thorn was regarded with a veneration that by the seventeenth century approached reverence. It was during the ascendancy of the fanatical element among the Puritans that it was cut down. Its executioners justified the vandalism by declaring the tree had become an object of idolatry. But the hawthorn is a tree of great virility. Soon new growths sprang up from the roots. From these, cuttings eventually were transplanted to all parts of the world, and it is said that many of them continued to blossom at Christmastide.

The gift to the National Cathedral was made in October, 1901. The famous ruins at Glastonbury were not then the property of the Church of England, but were owned by Stanley Austin, son of the then Poet Laureate of England, who sent the cutting to the Right Rev. Henry Yates Satterlee, first Bishop of Washington. At that time ground had not yet been broken

The Glastonbury Thorn planted in 1902 in the Close of the National Cathedral was a cutting from the original 'Holy Thorn' at Glastonbury Abbey, Somerset, England. It was presented to the National Cathedral by Stanley Austin, son of the then Poet Laureate of England. (Photo: Courtesy the National Cathedral)

for the Cathedral and plans were still incomplete. Mr. Austin also presented enough stone from the ancient Abbey to build a Bishop's Chair or Cathedra for the new edifice in Washington.

Significantly enough, the motif of the Glastonbury Thorn has a place in the National Cathedral's symbolic decorations. It is traced—leaf, seed pod, and blossoms—in the reredos of the Bethlehem Chapel's altar, and is again represented in one of the chapel's carved bosses.

Traditions have a way of expanding to include favored persons. Enduring from medieval times is the legend that whenever a member of England's royal family visits Glastonbury, the thorn puts forth blossoms. It was the custom to pluck a bud, place it in a silver box, and present it to the royal visitor. In November, 1919, the National Cathedral had an opportunity to perpetuate this tradition when the present Duke of Windsor paid his respects to the Bishop of Washington. On Christmas, 1918, the thorn had blossomed on Christmas Day for the first time since its planting. This was a date to remember—a season when "peace comforted the war-saddened earth." That memorable and significant blossoming of the holy thorn in 1918 was repeated at Christmastide in 1923 and again in 1948.

When Princess Elizabeth, the present Queen Elizabeth II, and the Duke of Edinburgh, now Prince Philip, visited the National Cathedral in November, 1951, the Glastonbury Thorn flowered for the royal visit and the ancient ceremony of presentation was carried out.

The thorn's traditional blooming for British royalty seemed due for its first failure when the Queen Mother attended a service in the Cathedral in November, 1954. Not a blossom could be found until the day before the arrival of Her Majesty, when the Rev. Canon Charles Martin, headmaster of St. Albans School for boys, found a blossom at the very top of the tree.

Upon arrival of Queen Elizabeth II and the royal party, October 20, 1957, the Glastonbury Thorn bloomed profusely. Instead of presenting the Queen with the blossoms, many flowering branches were included in the large floral displays used in the Cathedral for the occasion. Queen Elizabeth and Prince Philip attended a special service of the dedication of the War Memorial Chapel in the National Cathedral.

Thus, this cherished plant tradition lives on through the centuries. A scion of the original Glastonbury Thorn, flourishing not far from our nation's Capitol, stands as a living symbol of an era when symbols were a more intimate part of the lives of men than they are today.

CHAPTER IV

Out of Paradise

"IN ADAM'S FALL, we sinned all." What a way to begin the story of the Christmas tree—the best loved and most glorious symbol of the most festive of seasons. This is no sermon from that stern Puritan divine Cotton Mather; actually the tree of trees as we know it, handed down through ten centuries of cherished tradition and custom, had its beginning in a medieval play about Adam and Eve, presented during Advent, the four weeks preceding Christmas. In those remote days it was the custom to commemorate the feast day of our first parents, which occurred on December 24. While the day was never officially observed in the Roman calendar, it was a cherished feast in the Eastern Church and the popularity of this special day became widespread among the populace throughout Europe.

Miracle and mystery plays as performed in the Middle Ages were the only means, aside from preaching, by which people could learn the truths of religion. The terms "miracle" and "mystery" used in connection with these pageants referred to the episodes of Christ's life as narrated in the Gospels. There were no printed books in those days and pictures were scarce. The illuminated manuscripts written in the monasteries were not available to the people at large.

When first presented, the plays given within the churches were in the Latin tongue. Serious and solemn in tone, they were largely patterned after the expanding liturgical service of the time and were sometimes performed during public worship. Gradually, the plays evolved from simple presentations with few props and no scenery to elaborate performances in which the number of characters increased. As laymen joined with the clergy, the individual plays were arranged in a lengthy series or cycle throughout the church year. Thus, they encompassed the Old and New Testaments, beginning with the story of creation and ending with the Resurrection.

The cycles given during Advent opened with Adam and Eve, followed by a scene built around the domestic difficulties of Noah and his wife, which always brought hearty laughter. Noah's wife was something of a scold who made life so difficult for the owner of the Ark that he went off into a corner to get out of the way. Cain and Abel made their appearance, followed by

Moses and David and King Solomon in all his glory. The appearance of the
shepherds heralded the birth of the Christ Child:

> Come and make a joyful sound,   He is come to dwell on earth,
> God with man henceforth is found.   As a Little Boy He's here.

Melchior, Gaspar, and Balthazar, the three Kings resplendent in rich robes,
added luster to the performance which came to a climax as Mary and Joseph
made their way into Egypt, fearing as they did the tyranny of King Herod.

With the rise of the vulgar tongue, whether it was English, French, or
German, the Latin used in the mystery plays gave way to a freer and easier
mode of expression. The use of the vernacular in these plays helped to develop the human qualities of the various characters portrayed. Creature comforts, human faults, touches of humor were woven into the various episodes.
The performances glowed with warmth and appeal as popular speech had full
play. Thus, from solemn religious ceremonial, a spirited kind of secular drama
developed. Since such pageants were hardly suited to the sanctuary of the
church, the performances were moved outdoors to the steps and yard of the
church, and eventually to the public square. This change occurred in the
fifteenth century.

Hundreds of vagabond scholars, known as goliards, traveled from teacher
to teacher and monastery to monastery in search of knowledge. Young, poor,
seeking adventure and excitement, they were eager to take part in the plays.
The outcome was reflected in the broadened outlook of these youths who gave
the plays a vital lifelike quality filled with action and sparkling dialogue.
Naturally, they took considerable license as they allowed their imaginations
free play.

As the plays grew in popularity, pagan elements were blended with Christian theology. Spiritual and materialistic influences appeared in strange contrast. Realism replaced allegory and broad, sometimes coarse, humor permeated
the ever-expanding cycles. They grew in length as episode after episode was
introduced. Soon it was found that the cold winter season was hardly suited
to these open-air performances, so they were held at Whitsuntide or on the
feast of Corpus Christi. Cycles known as the Towneley, Chester, and Coven-
try were named for the towns where they originated and the players traveled
about to give performances in neighboring communities.

Particularly suited to the Christmas season was the Paradise play, dramatiz-
ing the episodes in the life of our first parents and their banishment from the
Garden of Eden. First there was the creation of man. The sin of Adam and
Eve was depicted when Eve gave Adam the apple which she plucked from
an evergreen tree.

The fir tree hung with apples representing the Garden of Eden was the only prop on stage, and naturally it attracted the attention of the spectators, particularly the children. It is not too much to surmise that both actors and children helped themselves to apples when no one was looking. In any event, this symbol became firmly planted in their minds. Religious painters of the time created allegorical pictures which became widely known. Since they portrayed the mysteries of the faith, the paradise tree was often reproduced.

In popularizing the episodes of the Bible in the lusty spirit of the times, abuses and irreverences of speech and action occurred, to the dismay of the bishops and other church authorities. For this reason, their performance was forbidden toward the end of the fifteenth century. Yet, in many parts of Europe the miracle and mystery plays endured until the Reformation. In remote communities some lasted even longer, and a few persist to this day, although greatly changed in dialogue.

Vivid memories of the fir tree decked with apples lived on long after the plays ceased to be performed in Germany. People then set these trees up in their homes to commemorate our first parents on their feast day, no doubt using them to convey the message of the Adam and Eve play to their children. The fir tree hung with apples was an evergreen. Being *ever green* it symbolized immortality. The apples which represented Adam's fall were the sign of sin. To these simple decorations, they added round wafers which signified the Sacred Host—the fruits of redemption.

The wafers on the *Christbaum* (as the tree is called in Germany) were replaced by cookies of various shapes and sizes. These flavorsome pastries made of white dough in the shapes of flowers, bells, stars, angels, and hearts and those of brown dough cut in the forms of men and various animals, were sheer delight to the children. Old cookie molds made of wood and tin were among the treasured heirlooms which the early German settlers brought to America in the 18th century.

But what of the lights on the Christmas tree? The candle as the prime source of light in those times was also the oldest of symbols. In fact, the very mention of candles for festive use on any of the feast days brings forth a host of recollections emanating from every corner of the world. Particularly significant for use at Christmas, the lighted candle as derived from liturgical usage represented Christ in all His glory—the Light of the World. Thus, candles were lighted with ceremony on Christmas Eve with all the members of the family participating. Again on Christmas night and continuing through the feast of Epiphany, the symbolic candles were burned.

In Germany, instead of a single candle many small ones were placed on a lightstock or pyramid made of shelves of graduated widths. When lighted, the effect was that of an elaborate candelabrum gleaming with cheerful flames on several levels. The name *Lichtstock* clearly defines the purpose of this

candlestand which was decorated with baubles and tinsel to give it a truly festive appearance.

The paradise tree and the lightstand or pyramid with its candles when combined produced what we know today as the Christmas tree. The history of this tree and the various customs associated with it, and the elaborate pyramidal candlestick, add up to a clearly defined concept of the tree, lighted with tapers and hung with apples and cookies.

What of the tradition of flowering trees (described in Chapter III) as used for decoration at Christmas, and the lore associated with them? Some students of folklore have claimed that the Christmas tree owes its origin to this custom which was fused with the older pre-Christian practice of adorning houses with greens during the Kalends of January. As evidence they cite the earliest record of a Christmas tree recorded at Strasbourg in 1605 "hung with roses cut from paper of many colors, apples, wafers, spangle-gold, sweets, etc." There was no mention of candles in this description but the record is incomplete since part of it was torn. However, apples and wafers were listed among the decorations, the basic ornaments of the Paradise tree.

Both the apples and the wafers (later cookies) had symbolic significance as used on the Paradise tree. "A rose for every candle" also had a special kind of meaning. Of all blossoms, the rose was the emblem of love and beauty, the queen of flowers dedicated to the Virgin Mary. Medieval and Renaissance painters portraying the Madonna used the rose as her symbol over and over again. What more appropriate decoration for the *Christbaum* than a rose—even one made of paper or cloth!

Thus, the Christmas tree had its origin among the inhabitants of Western Germany on the left border of the Rhine. The Paradise tree, in the form of a fir tree, with its evergreen needles and pyramidal habit of growth, was similar in shape to the wooden pyramid which held the candles. Both were set up in the best room of the house on the same day of the year, December 24. The two when combined made an ornamental symbol gleaming with light to teach the children that Christ was the Light of the World. The star from the pyramid was placed at the top of the tree and a Christmas crib was set up at the base or near it. This picture needed no words to convey its message. Father Weiser reminds us in his *Handbook of Christian Feasts and Customs* that fir boughs and trees decorated in the manner described above are still found in sections of Bavaria where they are known as *Paradeis*.

In many parts of Central Europe the pyramid is still used side by side with the Christmas tree. At first glance, a pyramid gives the impression of a curious kind of Christmas what-not, reminiscent of those Victorian stands for bric-a-brac used in parlors. Shelves of varying sizes, either triangular, square, or many-sided, fastened to light wooden poles, were decorated with

The Christmas pyramid, forerunner of the Christmas tree in Germany, was often elaborately decorated. In Italy it was called a ceppo and contained many of the cherished family mementoes associated with the most festive of holidays. The making of these decorative stands was often a family hobby and some of them, hexagonal or octagonal in shape, were operated mechanically so that they revolved when the candles were lighted

sprigs of evergreen. Candles, pictures, and little figurines were placed on them. The custom was known in Germany, Italy, and England. In Herefordshire they were decorated with gilded evergreens, apples, and nuts, and were carried about by the children as gifts to be offered at Christmas or on the New Year. Those who enjoy collecting *objets d'art* in miniature still find them fascinating for Christmas decoration. They often serve today as a setting for a tiny crèche, a group of angels, or other figurines suited to the season. Mementos of Christmas, keepsakes, and even greeting cards can be used to adorn the pyramid.

In Italy, the pyramid was called a *ceppo,* which actually means a log, and may have been a substitute for the old practice of decorating and burning the Yule log at Christmas. Usually there was one for each child in the family, since they were easy to make and inexpensive. In the delightful book entitled *The Florentine Christmas of a Century Ago,* by E. A. Tribe, we find this picturesque description:

"These curious pyramidal constructions of cardboard were made on a framework of three or four laths, or canes from one-and-a-half to three feet high. They were crossed with transverse shelves of wood or cardboard rising to three or four stories, according to size, and the whole covered with colored paper with fringes and tufts and tassels, and ornamented with little gilt pine cones symmetrically arranged. At the bottom of the pyramid was placed a much larger gilt pine cone or a puppet, and along the sides of the pyramid were lighted wax tapers and little flags of many colors. The shelves on which the smaller presents were placed were covered with moss or colored paper. The lowest storey often contained in the center the cradle, with the Infant Jesus in wax or plaster, surrounded by shepherds, saints and angels. The *ceppi* sold already ornamented but without presents; these were left to the choice and generosity of the parents and friends, who secretly brought to the house their contributions of toys, sweets and fruits."

The pyramid in various elaborate forms was for the tradesmen and artisans of the time an ideal kind of Christmas symbol. Made of wood, it could be kept from year to year. Thus, precious young forest trees were not wasted in lands where conservation of timber trees has long been an established practice. In fact, the Christmas pyramid is a most practical kind of decoration and has unlimited possibilities for present-day use. It can be fitted up in any number of ways to make a striking table or floor decoration, depending on its size. Pyramids are fun to make and the shelves can be three- or five-sided, round, or have six, seven, or eight sides, according to one's fancy.

CHAPTER V

The Christmas Tree in Germany

THE "CHRISTMAS-KEEPING GERMANS," as Michael Harrison calls them, have made of the Christmas tree their country's symbol of the season and "through their own loyalty and a foreigner's love of the exotic, disseminated its worship throughout the world." In this country of countless acres of forests, a celebration centered around an evergreen seems to belong, for as Clement Miles has expressed it, the tree "is a kind of sacrament linking mankind to the mysteries of the forest." But there is another kind of sacramental significance expressed. Earlier generations of Germans had cherished the tree of the miracle and mystery plays and they adopted this Paradise tree for their own very special hearthside observance of Christmas. Thus they perpetuated an old religious symbol, separate and distinct from the Yule tree with which the Christmas tree is sometimes linked.

Many attempts have been made to associate the Christmas tree with the more ancient Yule tree of German and Scandinavian folklore. It was a custom to place an evergreen, called a Yule tree, at the entrance, or in the dooryard, or to plant a small specimen in a tub and bring it indoors. This use of a live tree with needles that were ever green, signifying immortality, helped to dispel the gloom of the long, dark cold days of winter. It served much the same kind of purpose as the foliage plants which we use for indoor winter decoration today. In fact, it was the fashion in Victorian times to grow a tropical evergreen known as the Norfolk Island Pine indoors during the winter months, along with the rubber plant and various kinds of palms.

In tracing the history and significance of trees through the ages and especially their use for decoration, it is not at all surprising to find that a small evergreen in a tub would flourish in the sparsely heated houses of medieval times, and even in those of later centuries. To peasant and burgher alike, it was an indication that nature, which supported all growing activity, was merely dormant and not dead. Such a tree was not decorated, it merely grew as something ever green. In his *Handbook of Christian Feasts and Customs* Francis X. Weiser states: "Yule trees may still be found in some sections of

central Europe, standing side by side with the Christmas tree in the homes of rural districts. Their symbolism has remained entirely separate and sharply distinguished from that of the Christmas tree." In the same tradition, trees have been used for generations in the churches of many denominations at Christmas for their decorative effect. The practice was common in Europe even before the Episcopalians introduced this custom in America in the eighteenth century.

In the twilight of the Victorian era, Henry Van Dyke wrote *The First Christmas Tree,* which records one of the oldest legends relating to the origin of the Christmas tree. This charming narrative, although little read today, tells how St. Boniface, earlier known as Wynfred, brought Christianity to Germany. Like so many of the early missionaries who went into strange lands to preach the Gospel, his was a life of hardship and privation.

His early work among the German people brought him recognition from Pope Gregory II, but he returned to his adopted country to find that the eldest son of the Chieftain Gundhar was to be sacrificed to the gods on Christmas Eve. A giant oak, sacred to their patron Thor, was to be the scene of the sacrifice. Boniface decided to destroy this pagan symbol in order to prove that the pagan deity was powerless. After one stroke with the axe, a wind toppled the mighty oak. The assembled throng was awed by what happened and asked Boniface for the word of God. Pointing to an evergreen which grew nearby, he replied: "This is the word, and this is the counsel. Not a drop of blood shall fall tonight, for this is the birth-night of the Saint Christ, Son of the All-Father and Saviour of the world. This little tree, a young child of the forest, shall be a home tree tonight. It is the wood of peace, for your houses are built of fir. It is the sign of endless life, for its branches are ever green. See how it points toward Heaven! Let this be called the tree of the Christ-Child; gather about it, not in the wild woods but in your homes; there it will shelter no deeds of blood, but loving gifts and lights of kindness."

The wood of the fallen oak was used to build a little monastery and a church dedicated to Saint Peter. The fir tree was cut, taken to the Gundhar's great hall, and set up for the observance of Christmas. This, according to the legend, was the first Christmas tree.

Another greatly loved and widely told story about the origin of the Christmas tree refers to Martin Luther. It is related that after wandering about on Christmas Eve under a bright clear sky illuminated by countless stars, he returned home and set up a tree for his children. He lighted the little evergreen with numerous candles to impress his children with the true meaning of Christ, the Light of the World who had so gloriously brightened the sky on that Christmas Eve. Since there is no documented record for this story, it has been relegated to the realm of tradition, but it could have happened. In fact, it might have transpired even though it was not recorded. Whatever the facts, the story lives on and gives color and meaning to the ever-growing garland of Christmas tree traditions.

"At Christmas fir trees are set up in the rooms at Strasbourg and hung with roses cut from paper of many colors, apples, wafers, spangle-gold, sugar, etc. It is customary to surround it with a square frame . . . and in front . . ." The rest of the account has been lost. This widely quoted reference is the first authentic detailed record of an actual Christmas tree. It was the inspiration used by the noted English artist Pauline Baynes, who painted a series of illustrations depicting the history of the Christmas tree for the 1958 Christmas issue of the *Illustrated London News*. They are reproduced in this book by permission of the Editor. An earlier record makes mention of the tree in German Alsace, dated 1521. However, there is no mention of lights in this brief reference, or in the Strasbourg account.

More than a century later, we read that not everyone was impressed with the beauty and the wonder of the Christmas tree. Dr. Johann Dannhauer, professor and preacher at Strasbourg Cathedral, expressed himself strongly about such frivolity in his ponderous book, *The Milk of the Catechism,* published in 1757. He wrote, "Whence comes the custom, I know not; it is child's play . . . Far better were it to point the children to the spiritual cedar-tree, Jesus Christ."

In 1737, Karl Gottfried Kissling of the University of Wittenburg told of a lady of his acquaintance providing a small tree for each of her sons and daughters, with lighted candles on or around the tree and presents laid out for them. The children were called in one by one to receive the gifts intended for them.

As early as 1755, a regulation pertaining to the forests of Salzburg forbade the taking of small evergreen trees or bushes from the forests. This would indicate that the Christmas tree was becoming a popular institution. The dour words of a preacher had but little effect, even when offered in printed form. Child's play or not, the custom was taking root literally and figuratively. City folk grew trees in boxes in their yards and kept them from year to year. They were taken to the basement before freezing time and brought into the best room in time for Christmas Eve.

Stilling wrote of Christmas trees lighted and covered with gilt nuts, sheep, dolls, dishes, fruit, confectionery, and figures of the Christ Child in 1740 at Nassau. There is a story told of a Swedish soldier who was badly wounded during the Thirty Years' War (1616-1648) and nursed back to health by a kindly German family in Leipzig. As a mark of gratitude, he set up a lighted tree in one of the churches in the city.

Jung, Goethe, and Schiller mentioned the tree in their writings before 1800. In a novel, *The Sorrows of Young Werther,* written by Goethe in 1774, the heroine Lotte decorated a Christmas tree "with fruits and sweetmeats and lighted it up with wax candles." Werther remarked that it would bring the children "such transports of joy". The setting was laid in Wetzlar, in the heart of the country from which many of the Hessian soldiers were recruited by George III. Hertha Pauli has told a charming story of the young poet Goethe who set up a tree in 1769 to the delight of the children and the puppy in the home of a wood engraver in Leipzig. At the time, Goethe was studying law and had already written several hundred poems.

Samuel Taylor Coleridge visited in Northern Germany in 1798 and wrote a letter to a friend in England describing the enchanting custom of the Christmas tree he had seen while visiting there. "On the evening before Christmas Day, one of the parlours is lighted up by the Children, into which the parents must not go; a great yew bough is fastened on the table at a little distance from the wall, a multitude of little tapers are fixed in the bough, but not so as to burn it till they are nearly consumed, and coloured paper, etc., hangs and flutters from the twigs. Under this bough the children lay out in great order the presents they mean for their parents, still concealing in their pockets what they intend for each other. Then the parents are introduced, and each presents his little gift; they then bring out the remainder one by one, from their pockets, and present them with kisses and embraces. Where I witnessed this scene there were eight or nine children, and the eldest daughter and the mother wept aloud for joy and tenderness; and the tears ran down the face of the father, and he clasped all his children so tight to his breast, it seemed as if he did it to stifle the sob that was rising within it. I was very much affected. The shadow of the bough and its appendages on the wall, and arching over on the ceiling, made a pretty picture."

The fashion for Christmas trees seems to have first captured the fancy of the well-to-do tradespeople in German cities and towns, and some writers record that the peasants were slow to adopt it. For example, the tree as we know it was little known to the Bavarian peasants a century ago. Part of the reason for the slow spread of its popularity may be attributed to the fact that it was a custom cherished by the Lutherans. Thus, its progress in Catholic areas of Germany was somewhat slow at first, but the universal appeal of the tree soon knew no limits of creed or station.

So popular did the custom become that in Munich, and doubtless elsewhere, the trees began to appear in cemeteries on Christmas Eve. The graves of the dead were decked "with holly and mistletoe and a little Christmas tree with gleaming lights, a touching token of remembrance, an attempt, perhaps, to give the departed a share in the brightness of the festival."

A little more than a century ago, when the Christmas tree was formally introduced in England by Prince Albert and was also being widely featured in various parts of America, the whole spirit surrounding the German *Tannenbaum* began to attract the attention of English and American writers. There was something about the romance and splendor of it that held them in wonder and awe. Thus, they wrote about this supreme symbol of Christmas at great length, and we have as an enduring part of the heritage of the Christmas tree a rich garland which literally glows with color and enthusiasm.

Anna C. Johnson and H. J. Whitling were among the early writers in the 1850's, and for half a century following well-known literary figures like Edward Everett Hale, his sister Susan, Mrs. Alfred Sedgwick, Blanche Howard, and many others were painting awe-inspiring pictures in words of the wondrous tree and all the preparations and ceremony associated with it. Little wonder that this German custom became so widespread, not only in Europe but also in America, making the tree truly synonymous with Christmas. "It is that childish open-hearted simplicity which . . . makes Christmas essentially German, or at any rate explains why it is that nowhere else in the world does it find so pure an expression."

The Christmas markets in the large towns and the shops in the smaller communities were sheer joy to the observers, and the Christ Market, as it was known in Nuremberg, was particularly famous. Toy shops with counters brimming over with every conceivable kind of horn and drum, jack-in-the-box, dolls of all sizes and types, games, hobby horses, wagons, steam trains, stuffed toys, and all those other objects of joy and pleasure best known to the realm of childhood were more colorful than Paradise could ever be. Shops of grocers and stationers vied for attention with their displays "of coloured tissue paper, the gold leaf for gilding the nuts and apples, the strings of blue and red glass beads, the packets of delicately tinted tapers, the candies as hard as quartz, the dried figs and prunes, all to be fastened to the Christmas trees."

What are those little stacks of "what appear to be stick brooms of dark brown, or black color, tied in the middle, and making a stiff brush at both ends? What special mission have these at a Christmas festival? They are for the *Pelznickels* to punish disobedient children." During the first week in December, it was the custom for *Pelznickel* to enter every home. He was the special terror of all the children, not only because of his unpleasant appearance, but also because he knew all their failings. It was his to make decision regarding those "deserving of a merry Christmas, or whether they must be punished by having no gifts, and be condemned to solitude during the time others are happy together." In the north he was known as *Knecht Ruprecht,* "a messenger of Christ, sent by Him to make these inquiries and promises." To those too young to understand that all these antics were a practical joke,

he was considered a true prophet, and their reactions were either of joy or deep sorrow. This custom was eventually softened or given up in some families because of the deep impression made on the young children especially.

On Christmas Eve, all was changed to joy when "a blooming maiden, dressed in white, who sometimes forgave those whom *Pelznickel* had condemned and then showered on them the treasures which their families had prepared for them."

More joy and mirth filled the air and children's voices grew louder as the tree, hidden from their sight until now, came into view as the door opened. Myriads of tapers cast a blaze of light that glistened on the shining tree ornaments and then was reflected in the beaming eyes of the children. Words have no place when the eyes of little ones literally dance within their heads. Gold and silver walnuts, trinkets, and miniature toys of every description, baubles and glitter, cakes and cookies and spangled confectionery, these and many other wonderful things would be enjoyed more closely after the presents were distributed. There on the tables they were, packages of all sizes, marked with the names of all the family. "But pleasure lives not to itself alone, for the sounds of joy go on increasing, as love seeks and finds what love has given, and the voice of thankful happiness is breathed from every moved heart."

O Christmas tree, O Christmas tree,
How lovely are your branches.
In summer sun, in winter snow,
A dress of green you always show,
O Christmas tree, O Christmas tree,
How lovely are your branches.

O Christmas tree, O Christmas tree,
With happiness we greet you.
When decked with candles once a year
You fill our hearts with Yuletide cheer,
O Christmas tree, O Christmas tree,
With happiness we greet you.

What has made the German concept of the Christmas tree all the more intriguing and captivating is the miniature landscape setting arranged around it. Called by various names, it is best described as a Christmas yard or garden. Perhaps more than any other feature of the tree, these extraordinary creations which were introduced to America by the Moravians more than a century ago are still a source of wonder and amazement to all who see them. Under the tree was a miniature landscape, formed of moss and trees of Lilliputian dimensions — mountains in the background, a valley and meadow, a silver brook, and little hills. The principal feature was a stable, and in the manger the Christ Child with the Mother, and Joseph watching by. Far off are the shepherds on their way to kneel down and worship Him, and above the star gleams that guides them to the spot. In the garden leaps and sparkles a little fountain, and horses, cows, and sheep are browsing in the fields.

An American woman, Blanche Howard, who spent Christmas in Hamburg, Germany, in 1876, has left a most charming account of her experiences on Christmas Eve in a little book entitled *One Year Abroad*.

The Lady of Wittenberg, 1737. This painting is based on an account of a German Christmas
party at which each child had its own tree surrounded with gifts. Specially drawn for *The Illustrated London News*, Christmas Number 1958, by Pauline Baynes

Christmas morning in a Continental drawing room about 1790

Christmas Eve in 19th-century Germany was something to remember

"Christmas in general is something about which there is nothing to say, because it sings its own songs without words in all our hearts; but a story of one particular Christmas may not be amiss here, since it tells of a pretty and graceful welcome in which Germans knew how to give to a wanderer — a welcome in which tones of tenderness were underlying the merriment, and delicate consideration shaped the whole plan.

"In a room radiant, not with one Christmas-tree, but with five — a whole one for each person being the generous allowance — stood a lordly fir, glistening with long icicles of glass, resplendent with ornaments of scarlet and gold and white. The stars and stripes floated proudly from its top; unmistakable cherries of that delectable substance, Marzipan, hung in profusion from its branches; and at its base stood the Father of his Country. George, on this occasion, was a doll of inexpressibly fascinating mien, arrayed in a violet velvet coat, white satin waistcoat and knee-breeches, lace ruffles, silver buckles, white wig, and three-cornered hat, and wearing that dignified, imperturbable Washingtonian expression of countenance which one would not have believed could be produced on a foreign shore. He held no hatchet in his hand, but graciously extended a document heavily sealed and tied with red, white, and blue ribbons.

"This document was written in elegant and impressive English. A very big and fierce-looking American eagle hovered over the page, which was also adorned by the arms of the German Empire and of Hamburg. The purport of the document was that George Washington, first President of the United States, did herewith present his compliments to a certain wandering daughter of America, wishing her, on the part of her country, family, and friends,

"A merry Christmas and happy New Year, and 'all foreign authorities, corporations, and private individuals were enjoined to promote, by all legal means of hospitality and goodwill, the loyal execution of the above-mentioned wishes.' It displayed the names of several highly honorable witnesses, and concluded: 'Given under my hand and seal at my permanent White House residence, Elysium, 24th December, 1876.

George Washington.'

"And the seal bore the initials of the mighty man.

"The tree yielded gifts many and charming, but the sweetest gift was the kindly thought that prompted the pretty device. Though one had to smile where all were smiling, yet was it not, all in all, quite enough to make one a little 'teary roun' the lashes,' especially when one is very much 'grown up,' and so has not the remotest claim upon the happy things that, 'by the grace of God,' belong to the children? Such scenes make one feel the world is surely not so black as it is painted."

The tree, for all its color and glamor, would hardly have captured the hearts of children and held them enraptured for the days before and those that followed Christmas were it not for the presents. Visions of the festive tree conjured up in their dreams, during those long hours of waiting in the days before Christmas, were built up around what they would receive. And the various helpers of the Christ Child who brought their gifts were very real to them in a wonderful sort of way.

In Roman times, people exchanged offerings of pastry, lamps, coins, and other tokens of good will on New Year's Day. Pastry was given with the wish that the year would be full of sweetness, lamps as the symbol of light, and coins for prosperity. With such an auspicious beginning, the year would be one of bounty, filled with the good things of life. An earlier practice involved the mere giving of branches picked from the grove of the goddess Strenia from which the name *strenae* came to be used for the more elaborate tokens of later years. This Roman custom survives today in France, where New Year's is the time for adults to exchange gifts. Bachelors paid their social debts by sending boxes of sweets to all who had entertained them during the year.

With the transfer of emphasis from New Year's to Christmas in early Christian times, the traditional gift-giving took on new meaning. The Christ Child, the giver of all good things spiritual and material, was the source of the earthly bounty that men sought. In most European countries it was the Child Jesus who brought the gifts at Christmas. The children were told the legend that on the eve of His birth a little child came with His angels to trim their trees and place their presents under it. In France, it was *le petit Jesus,* in Germany *Christkind* or *Christkindel,* from which the name was eventually changed to Kriss Kringle. Thus gifts were known as "Christ bundles" and contained all the things that children enjoyed eating, playing with, and using. The gifts were given on the basis of good behavior, and so, as this custom developed there arose the idea of a reward to good children and punishment for the bad. Thus, children at an early age were introduced to the basic tenets of theology.

But what of Saint Nicholas, the fourth-century Bishop of Myra whose feast was celebrated on December 6 in the season of Advent? He was a bringer of gifts some three weeks before Christmas to those who merited them. His fame spread over Europe in the Middle Ages and the strange story of his life was told and retold. He became the patron of cities and whole countries as well as of bakers, merchants, and sailors. Most of all he was the beloved inspiration of children for he was their special patron.

Orphaned at an early age, he decided when he became a young man to dedicate his life to God by aiding the poor and unfortunate. Great and numerous were his acts of kindness, always carried out without fanfare or display, and often his identity was not known. His travels took him to the Holy Land and finally, when his greatness was discovered, he was made Bishop of Myra. In those early days, many Christian leaders were persecuted and Nicholas was among them, but he survived to return to his bishopric where he continued his saintly life and his abounding charity. After his death

The Christmas tree market in Leipsic teemed with excitement

a great church was built in his memory, and because of his noble deeds there was widespread devotion to him and his feast was observed annually. His appearance on December 6 served to prepare the children for the feast of Christmas.

With the many changes that occurred at the time of the Reformation, the spirit of St. Nicholas was transferred to the jolly character who was known successively as Father Christmas, the Christmas Man, *Papa Noel* (in France), *Pelznickel* and other titles in Germany, and finally Santa Claus (from the Dutch *Sinter Klaas*). Christmas instead of December 6 (the feast of St. Nicholas) became the time for receiving presents. The enchanting story of Santa Claus, whose existence dates back only a few centuries, has all the overtones of a curious kind of fantasy that stemmed from a simple and beautiful tradition of the Middle Ages.

Winter, inspired by The Marriage of Figaro

Distributing Christmas Gifts, 1799

Early German Christmas tree and pyramids

They're "Sold out," the sign reads

CHAPTER VI

The Custom Is Transplanted to England

THE CHRISTMAS after his first son was born, Prince Albert, Queen Victoria's consort from the German province of Saxe-Coburg, entertained his children with an elaborate Christmas tree at Windsor Castle. Seven years later, in 1848, the *Illustrated London News* featured this newly introduced custom in its Christmas Supplement with a full-page engraving and a description of the eight-foot fir tree with its six tiers of branches. "On each tier, or branch, are arranged a dozen wax tapers. Pendent from the branches are elegant trays, baskets, bonbonnières, and other receptacles for sweetmeats, of the most varied and expensive kind; and of all forms, colours, and degrees of beauty. Fancy cakes, gilt gingerbread and eggs filled with sweetmeats, are also suspended by variously-coloured ribbons from the branches."

Not even the minutest detail was omitted in recording this important observance in the Queen's household. "The tree, which stands upon a table covered with white damask, is supported at the root by piles of sweets of a larger kind, and by toys and dolls of all descriptions, suited to the youthful fancy, and to the several ages of the interesting scions of Royalty for whose gratification they are displayed. The name of each recipient is affixed to the doll, bonbon, or other present intended for it, so that no differences of opinion in the choice of dainties may arise to disturb the equanimity of the illustrious juveniles. On the summit of the tree stands the small figure of an angel, with outstretched wings, holding in each hand a wreath." Here was a charming new idea for Christmas which Victoria's subjects could adopt for their own in every cottage and castle in the land. And they did.

Actually, it was not a completely new idea in England, since German settlers had brought this cherished tradition with them several decades earlier, and members of the British royal family in previous generations had known and enjoyed the tree. Yet this Teuton novelty had little appeal for the rank and file, or even for middle-class families. About this time, the Christmas tree had become immensely popular in Germany, and wherever

men and women of German birth traveled, they introduced their beloved custom. To them, Christmas Eve was not complete or even fittingly observed without it. Decorated trees also had their place in the churches of the German settlers at the time.

What captivated the British was this symbolic picture of the royal family gathered around a fanciful illuminated tree which bespoke the essence of domestic tranquillity and peace. Neither German customs nor the Prince Consort himself were popular at the time. Yet Queen Victoria had given birth to a son, the Prince of Wales, and her family life was developing the pattern her subjects so much desired. The tree became English overnight. Despite the fact that Prince Albert did not win the hearts of England, he made many notable contributions to the English way of life and not the least of these was the Christmas tree. In a letter to his father he wrote: "To-day I have two children of my own to give presents to, who, they know not why, yet feel a happy wonder at the German Christmas-tree and its radiant candles." The reaction on the other side of the Atlantic a few years later was equally warm when the illustration, somewhat changed in detail, was used to set the fashion in America in *Godey's Lady's Book*.

Nor was the tree a new idea to the young Victoria. She had known of the custom at the age of thirteen as recorded in her diary for December 24, 1832. "After dinner we went upstairs. Aunt Sophia came also. We went into the drawing-room near the dining room. There were two large round tables on which were placed the trees hung with lights and sugar ornaments. All the presents being placed around the tree. I had one table for myself and the Conroy family had the other together." After listing her gifts and the donors, she added in little-girl fashion, "I stayed up until ½ past 9." Aunt Sophia was one of six daughters of Princess Victoria's great-aunt, Queen Charlotte, wife of George III.

At court Queen Charlotte had to plan many fetes and entertainments, as well as celebrations for numerous religious and national holidays and the birthdays of her thirteen children. These have been described elaborately in diaries and memoirs, but the family Christmas parties, kept in true German fashion at Windsor, were feasts of the heart shared only by those around the hearth and such cousins and friends who might be visiting. Queen Charlotte loved Christmas and her family observance of the day was planned around the Christmas tree.

At her death in 1819, her personal life was reviewed by Dr. John Watkins who remembered the royal Christmases of the late 1700's. "Sixty poor families had a substantial dinner given them; and in the evening the children of the principal families in the neighbourhood were invited to an entertainment at the Lodge. Here, among other amusing objects for the gratifications of the juvenile visitors, in the middle of the room stood an immense tub with a yew

Queen Caroline's Christmas tree in the 1820's was an evergreen bough set up for the delight of the household. Specially drawn for *The Illustrated London News*, Christmas Number 1958, by Pauline Baynes

Prince Albert, Queen Victoria, and the Royal family at Windsor Castle. *The Illustrated London News,* 1848

tree placed in it, from the branches of which hung bunches of sweetmeats, almonds, and raisins in papers, fruits, and toys, most tastefully arranged, and the whole illuminated by small wax candles."

There are several other accounts of trees set up for titled families including one by Baron Bunsen at Hanover in 1838 and another by the Swiss governess in the family of Baroness Bloomfield. In 1831, Lord Ravensworth and his family enjoyed a Christmas tree in Durham. Among the writings of Charles Dickens are references to the Christmas trees and the gifts he received when he was a child. Dickens was born in 1811 and the Christmas tree which he referred to as a German toy in 1850 was actually an old acquaintance.

In the time of Henry VIII, elaborate banquets, pageants, and fetes were an important part of the Christmas observance, which lasted until Epiphany. A pageant presented at Court in 1516 had a mountain made of stones on the top of which was a tree of gold with great spreading branches ornamented with roses and pomegranates. The richly decked tree was only a part of the setting to create the illusion of luxury, and was a far cry from the simple Christmas trees set up in Alsace a few years later (1521). However, the use of roses and pomegranates as decorations is significant. This and other proto-types of the Christmas tree, found in old documents, serve to impress us with the fact that trees had more than casual association with the lives of men in all stations of life.

"Against the feast of Christmas, every man's house, as also their parish churches, were decked with holme (holly) ivy, bayes, and whatsoever the season of the year afforded to be green. The conduits and standards in the streets were likewise garnished; among the which I read that, in the year 1444, by tempest of thunder and lightning, towards the morning of Candle-mas Day, at the Leadenhall in Cornhill, a standard of tree, being set up in the midst of the pavement (roadway) faste in the ground, nailed full of holme and ivy, for disport of Christmas to the people, was torne up and cast down by the malignant spirit (as was thought), and the stones of the pavement all about were cast in the streets, and into divers houses, so that the people were sore aghast at the great tempests." This account from Stow's *Survey of London* published late in the fifteenth century is prime evidence of the custom of decorating, and not the least important part of the description is the tree set up in the roadway. A kind of Christmas tree in the broad sense of the word, this outdoor ornament was undoubtedly another expression of the Yule tree of earlier days.

On Christmas day in Yorkshire, the wassail-bob or wesley-bob was carried about with ceremony. This was a bunch of holly and other greens fashioned like a bower, hung with apples and oranges and colored ribbons. Sometimes a pair of dolls ornamented with ribbons were nestled in the branches. Most

likely they were made of beeswax to represent the Virgin Mary and the Child Jesus.

In Westmoreland it used to be the custom on Twelfth Night to carry a holly tree decked with torches through the countryside in the early evening. Tiny trees made of holly and other evergreens were fastened to poles and carried by carol singers during the Christmas season as they went from house to house.

Children singing carols on Christmas morning in Yorkshire

A curious kind of bower that utilized some of the decorations associated with the Christmas tree in combination with figures from the Christmas Crib is the kissing ball, or kissing bunch. This sphere of evergreens and holly berries derived its name from the cluster of mistletoe suspended from it. A curious and handsome ornament, it had one prime purpose. Like the Christmas tree, it was the center of holiday festivities in cottage or hall, and was known long before the tree came to England. When hung, it was the source of great merriment until it was finally dismantled. The presence of the mistletoe which was suspended from the green sphere was all the license needed for a lad to grasp the girl of his choice, or any comely maid who happened to appear, and whisk her under it to bestow a kiss.

It involved a little effort to make a kissing bunch, for it "is always an elaborate affair. The size depends upon the couple of hoops — one thrust

Kissing ball made with wire hoops and decorated with artificial fruit and holly berries. A candle was placed in the center and a cluster of fresh mistletoe gives it meaning. Arranged by Mrs. Edward Woll in the Claflin Richards House, Wenham Historical Association

through the other — which form its skeleton. Each of the ribs is garlanded with holly, ivy, and sprigs of other greens, with bits of coloured ribbons and paper roses, rosy-cheeked apples, specially reserved for this occasion, and oranges. Three small dolls are also prepared, often with much taste, and these represent our Saviour, the mother of Jesus, and Joseph. These dolls generally hang within the kissing bunch by strings from the top, and are surrounded by apples, oranges tied to strings, and various brightly coloured ornaments. Occasionally, however, the dolls are arranged in the kissing bunch to represent a manger-scene . . . Mistletoe is not very plentiful in Derbyshire; but, generally, a bit is obtainable, and this is carefully tied to the bottom of the kissing bunch, which is then hung in the middle of the house-place, the centre of attention during Christmastide."

This description from the folk records of Derbyshire inspired the making of many a kissing bunch, especially in Victorian times when the custom was revived on both sides of the Atlantic. Then this elaborate contraption was somewhat forgotten and people were content to merely hang a spray of mistletoe from the chandelier or over a door. But the kissing bunch is coming into its own again as many age-old customs are being revived. So it's "up again with the old kissing bunch."

In the thirteenth century Saint Francis brought new meaning to the observance of Christmas when he dramatized the human side of the birth of

Potted evergreens were fashionable in Covent Garden Market a century ago

Christ. Six centuries later, the Victorian era rediscovered Christmas for all the world, adding as its contribution a warm humanitarian approach to the festivities of the season. And the Christmas tree, laden with ornaments and surrounded with gifts, became its symbol, perhaps best expressed in that beloved story, *The Christmas Tree,* written by Charles Dickens in 1855. Today, a century after its first appearance in printed form, it remains fresh and delightful, warm and personal, filled with sentiment and nostalgia. Some of the toys described may seem a bit old-fashioned and out-of-date but they are for all of us a kind of peepshow of memory.

"I have been looking on, this evening, at a merry company of children assembled round that pretty German toy, a Christmas Tree. The tree was planted in the middle of a great round table, and towered high above their heads. It was brilliantly lighted by a multitude of little tapers; and everywhere sparkled and glittered with bright objects. There were rosy-cheeked dolls, hiding behind the green leaves; there were real watches (with moveable hands, at least, and an endless capacity of being wound up) dangling from innumerable twigs; there were French-polished tables, chairs, bed-steads, wardrobes and eight-day clocks, and various other articles of domestic furniture (wonderfully made, in tin, at Wolverhampton), perched among the boughs, as if in preparation for some fairy housekeeping; there were jolly, broad-faced little men, much more agreeable in appearance than many real men — and no wonder, for their heads took off, and showed them to be full of sugar-plums; there were fiddles and drums; there were tambourines, books, work-boxes, paint-boxes, sweetmeat-boxes, peep-show boxes, all kinds of boxes; there were trinkets for the elder girls, far brighter than any group-up gold and jewels; there were baskets and pin-cushions in all devices; there were guns, swords, and banners; there were witches standing in enchanted rings of paste-board, to tell fortunes; there were tee-totums, humming-tops, needle-holders; real fruit, made artificially dazzling with gold leaf; imitation apples, pears, and walnuts, crammed with surprises; in short, as a pretty child, before me, delightedly whispered to another pretty child, her bosom friend, 'There was everything, and more.'

"This motley collection of odd objects, clustering on the tree like magic fruit, and flashing back the bright looks directed towards it from every side — some of the diamond-eyes admiring it were hardly on a level with the table, and a few were languishing in timid wonder on the bosoms of pretty mothers, aunts and nurses — made a lively realization of the fancies of childhood; and set me thinking how all the trees that grow and all the things that come into existence on the earth, have their wild adornments at that well-remembered time."

Christmas morning, 1873, from *Harper's Monthly*

CHAPTER VII

The Christmas Tree Takes Root in America

CHRISTMAS in the early days of the Colonies had its ups and downs even before the heavy hand of Cromwell forbade its observance in England. Governor Bradford at Plymouth nearly had a sitdown strike on his hands in December, 1621. Some of his men refused to work and he tolerantly granted them the day off, stating that "if they made it a matter of conscience, he would spare them till they were better informed." However, he soon discovered that they were playing ball in the street and that was too much for Bradford. Like so many of his contemporaries, his viewpoint was colored by the abuses of the Christmas celebrations he had seen at home. Several decades later Cotton Mather was to sum it up in his tirade against "revelling, dicing, carding, masking, mumming."

Even before Mather denounced Christmas, the General Court of Massachusetts had levied its stamp of disapproval on the popish holiday. In May, 1659, there was enacted a statute "for preventing disorders." Its contents are worth reading.

"For preventing disorders arising in several places within this jurisdiction by reason of some still observing such festivities as were superstitiously kept in other communities, to the great dishonor of God's and offense to others;

"Therefore that whosoever shall be found observing any such day as Christmas or the like, either by forbearing of labor, feasting, or any other way upon any such account aforesaid, every such person so offending shall pay for every offense five shillings as a fine to the county."

Curiously enough, the law was repealed in 1681 on the advice of the Attorney General—a good ten years before the horrible outbreak of "witch hunting" in Salem. Yet during the ensuing century in New England there was little widespread observance of Christmas. In 1685, Judge Sewell, a vigorous Puritan, was still bursting with indignation when he wrote: "Some somehow observe the day, but are vexed, I believe, that the Body of the People Profane it; and, blessed be God, no Authority yet to compel them to keep it."

Flags were popular decorations on this tree shown in *Godey's Lady's Book*, 1866

In marked contrast, the gay Dutch in New York made a well-rounded celebration of Christmas. They observed the feast of St. Nicholas on December 6, and the principal days, three weeks later, were recognized by closing public offices, holding elaborate church services and a full quota of festivity. There were Puritans in this colony too, but this did not deter the Dutch. Likewise, in Pennsylvania there were marked differences in the celebration of Christmas. For the Moravians at Bethlehem it was one of quiet but elaborate devotion, coupled with the restrained sociability which accompanied their love feast. But the Quakers, the Presbyterians, the Methodists, the Baptists, and the plain Dutch groups which included the Mennonites, Brethren, and Amish, would have no part of such popish nonsense. But Christmas as the Lutherans and the Reformed church groups had known it in their homeland was kept with all its traditions. Also, members of the Episcopal and Catholic churches observed the season to the fullest.

For those who kept Christmas, the liturgy in all its beauty was blended with a variety of traditions including carols, feasting, barring out the schoolmaster, and numerous other festive activities, including games, which were sometimes disturbing to those who did not observe the day.

Christmas in the South was observed annually as it had been at home in England, Germany, and France for centuries. In fact, many ancient customs,

from carol singing to mummering, feasting, and hunting, all colored by serenading and skylarking with firecrackers, have been kept alive in remote sections of the South with its rich and varied cultural background. Despite Spanish influence, the French settlers of New Orleans preserved their precious traditions intact. In Virginia the observance lasted for the full period from Christmas Eve to Epiphany and often overflowed well into January. The Moravians of North Carolina had their quiet and dignified love feast, which stood out in marked contrast to that of their roistering neighbors in nearby towns and adjoining states. Florida can lay claim to the earliest observance of Christmas in America, citing the visit of Hernando De Soto in 1539. Then there is the account of a Christmas observance at St. Augustine in 1565. John Bartram, noted Philadelphia botanist, described his Christmas among the Indians near Mobile in 1777. The French who settled Missouri in the 1730's firmly established the observance of both Christmas and New Year's Day. Harnett Kane in his lively volume, *The Southern Christmas Book,* has painted a brilliant and kaleidoscopic picture of this whole country where the spirit of Christmas was never dimmed, even during the Civil War.

The capital city of Washington is rich in anecdotes of Christmas observances at the White House from the time of Washington on. It is significant that the first three states to establish Christmas as a legal holiday were in the South — Alabama in 1836, followed by Louisiana and Arkansas in 1838.

Christmas morning in a Victorian parlor

Earliest illustration of the Christmas tree in America from *The Stranger's Gift* by Herman Bokum, printed in Boston 1836

Luther's family around the Christmas tree, painted in 1845 by Carl A. Schwerdgeburth

Did a celebration around a Christmas tree on a bitter cold Christmas Eve at Trenton, New Jersey, turn the tide for Colonial forces in 1776? From General Washington's diary we get a clear picture of that eventful December night. "Christmas, 6:00 P.M. It is fearfully cold and raw, and a snowstorm setting in. The wind is northeast and beats in the faces of the men. It will be a terrible night for the soldiers who have no shoes. Some of them have tied old rags around their feet, but I have not heard a man complain." In planning his strategy, Washington was as fully aware of the German custom of celebrating Christmas as he was of the fact that the day was not generally observed in the Colonies at the time. Furthermore, there was nothing available for his ragged soldiers to use. Nor was there anything about which to be festive. However, the Hessians had begun their festivities the previous evening.

Is it true that a little evergreen decked with candles to remind them of home so captured their hearts that the Hessians, indulging in too much grog and feasting, left their posts unguarded? This is the charming story that has been told and retold for a hundred years or more. There is no documentary evidence to support it. Undoubtedly, the Hessian soldiers were familiar with the Christmas tree that was so popular at home. They hailed from a province on the opposite side of the Rhine in which the custom originated. It could have happened, and in fact it may have been the real reason.

Historians dismiss the story as fiction, a figment of somebody's imagination. Yet, as William J. Schreiber of Wooster, Ohio, points out, Goethe described a Christmas tree in his novel, *The Sorrows of Young Werther,* written in 1774. The scene of the story is the "Hessian" country, and the custom of the tree is referred to as though it were well known.

Among other places where the Hessians made their presence felt was Newport, Rhode Island. This thriving seaport, then known as the "Intellectual Constellation of the Western Hemisphere," was torn asunder with the arrival of several thousand German mercenaries and an equal number of British troops in 1776.

At first the inhabitants were fearful of the Hessians and shied away from them, declaring that these Germans mercenaries ate up little children. However, they soon learned to understand the broken English of the Hessians and a better feeling developed. These handsome foreigners were billeted in their homes as well as in dwellings vacated by the prominent Tories, who had left their Newport homes before the British occupied the town. Some of these soldiers spent three Christmases away from home. In their endeavor to keep alive the cherished customs of their homeland, they introduced many of them to the Rhode Island Puritans who had a broader outlook on life than their Massachusetts neighbors. Tradition has it that they set up Christmas trees

for the Newport children. Cora Cheney Partridge has told the story in a charming book called *The Christmas Tree Hessian.* However, no documentary evidence has been found to support this tradition.

Some years earlier, in 1747, the Moravian settlers had celebrated their beloved feast of Christmas, using pyramids made of wood. From the diary of one of the Moravian brethren we read: "Quite early, the little children enjoyed a delightful festal occasion. Their brethren had decorated various pyramids with candles, apples, and hymn stanzas and, also, drawn a picture in which the children were represented as presenting their Ave to the Christ Child, all of which Brother Johannes (de Watteville) explained to them in a childlike manner, so that the love-feast conducted for them at the same time had a very blessed effect upon them as well as upon all the brethren and sisters present." The Christmas pyramid which served originally as a type of candlestand was then popular in Germany and other parts of Europe.

Another early account tells of a Christmas tree enjoyed by the soldiers of Fort Dearborn, Michigan, in 1804. Captain Whistler, a native of Ireland, "ordered a tree from the grove of pine and spruce on the hills that skirted the lake to the mouth of the river." The story tells how some of the soldiers dragged it with ropes across the icy river to its place of honor among the festivities. It is claimed that he learned about Christmas trees from the Hessian soldiers. Yet fairly exhaustive research has turned up no actual records to support this claim.

The trail of the Christmas tree in Pennsylvania is a long and fascinating one and has engaged the attention of several noted scholars for a period of more than forty years. However, it has remained for Dr. Alfred L. Shoemaker, of the Pennsylvania Folklore Society, to weave the threads of the story together from material he has gathered from local newspapers and diaries. His recent book, *Christmas in Pennsylvania,* is a folk culture study of the Christmas customs of the Pennsylvania Germans. It contains a most complete and well-documented account of the introduction of the Christmas tree, filled with local color and delightful humor, and reads like a novel.

"Sally and our Thos. and Wm. Hensel was out for Christmas trees, on the hill at Kendrick's saw mill." This brief entry, probably the first record of the custom of going out to cut a Christmas tree in America, was recorded in his diary by Matthew Zahm, of Lancaster County. The date was December 20, 1821. Another diary reference unearthed recently makes mention of a tree set up at Easton, Pennsylvania, in 1816.

In the York *Gazette* of December 23, 1823, a curious and amusing notice appeared entitled "Society of Bachelors." The announcement told of a meeting to be held at which "the Old Maids have determined to present us with at least one Cart load of Ginger-cakes the society in turn therefore intend fixing Krischtkintle Bauhm [literally Kriss Kringle Tree in Pennsylvania Dutch] for the amusement of such as may think proper to give them a call. Its decorations shall be superb, superfine, superfrostical, shnockagastical, double refined, mill' twill'd made of Dog's Wool, Swingling Tow, and Posnum fur; which cannot fail to gratisfy taste."

Simon Snyder Rathvon, a noted Lancaster county scientist and scholar, recorded his reminiscences in the Lancaster *Intelligencer* in 1881. He wrote, "There are phantoms of humble little Christmas trees dancing through my mind that belong to periods from one to five years anterior to sixty years ago. During the winter of 1822 and 1823 I was a member of a farmer's family in the township of Donegal, and then first participated in the erecting of a Christmas tree after the 'country fashion' of that period."

Rudolf Hommel, who wrote a pamphlet entitled *On the Trail of the First Christmas Tree,* made reference to a tree set up in Harrisburg, Pennsylvania, by Reverend George Lochman, the pastor of Zion Lutheran Church in Harrisburg from 1815 to 1826. The Philadelphia *Saturday Evening Post,* December 10, 1825, described "trees visible through the windows, whose green boughs are laden with fruit, richer than the golden apples of the Hesperides, or the sparkling diamonds that clustered on the branches in the wonderful cave of Aladdin."

Obviously, Dr. Constantin Hering's tree set up in Philadelphia in 1834 was not the first in that city, but he was long credited with its introduction there. Born in a community near Leipzig, Germany, the young doctor arrived in the City of Brotherly Love in 1833. A longing for his beloved symbol of Christmas prompted him to go with his friend Freidrich Knorr to the woods on the Jersey side of the Delaware to cut evergreens. They carried the trees on their shoulders through the streets, causing considerable excitement among the children whom they met. Once the tree was set up, the doctor designated certain evenings when his patients and friends could come and see the tree. For fifty years, he carried on this custom.

A letter telling of Christmas in a boys' school in Philadelphia in 1841 described the tree as a novelty which was "decorated with coats of arms of the boys, fanciful designs and ribands."

The term Christmas Tree appeared apparently for the first time in print in a York, Pennsylvania, paper in 1830. The Dorcas Society of York, a group of ladies given to charity, published a notice in the local paper inviting people to an exhibition of fancy articles and the display of a famous Christmas tree. Six and a quarter cents was the price of the tickets, which would admit the public to see the wonderful tree.

Dr. Alfred L. Shoemaker paints a pleasant picture of the growing popularity of the Christmas tree in Pennsylvania. "In the 1840's the Christmas tree began

Charles Follen

H. Martineau

to become more or less commonplace. Literary pieces, alluding to the custom of putting up trees at Christmas, began to appear with some regularity each returning Christmas season. The very popular and widely advertised, children's book, *Kriss Kringle's Christmas Tree*, published in 1845 in Philadelphia, brought a pictorial representation and knowledge of the Christmas tree and Kriss Kringle to children all over the Nation. Trees started going up everywhere in the State, from Philadelphia to Pittsburgh . . .

"By 1840, the Christmas tree had moved to the advertising columns of the local press. *Kriss Kringle's Christmas Tree* gave this charming explanation in its introduction, the kind of message we find on book jackets today. "Fashions change, and of late Christmas Trees are becoming more common than in former times. The practice of hanging up stockings in the chimney corner for Kriss Kringle to fill with toys, pretty books, bon-bons, etc., for good children, and rods for naughty children, is being superseded by that of placing a Christmas Tree on the table to await the annual visit of the worthy Santa Klaus. He has, with his usual good nature, accommodated himself to this change in the popular taste; and having desired a literary gentleman to prepare his favourite Christmas present in accordance with this state of things, the following volume is the result of the new arrangement, and all parents, guardians, uncles, aunts, and cousins, who are desirous to conform to the most approved fashion, will take care to hang one, two, or a dozen copies of the book on their Christmas Tree for 1847."

Until recently, it was believed that the oldest documented record of a Christmas tree set up in America was of one which Charles Follen decorated for his son in Boston in 1832. Follen was a political refugee from Germany who came to America, learned the language and applied his scholarly background to the teaching of German at Harvard College. He married into a prominent Boston family and became active in the community. He made friends with many noted people of the day, among them Harriet Martineau, a noted economist, novelist, and anti-slavery champion from England.

It was his keen interest in the anti-slavery movement, some thirty years before the Civil War, that caused Mr. Follen's dismissal from Harvard. It caused great dismay among his friends, for he had received his appointment through the influence of Lafayette with the recommendation of George Ticknor, leading public figure in Boston. His memoirs, published in 1842 by his wife, gave the account of a Christmas tree observance held in honor of Miss Martineau at the Follen home in Milton. She, too, wrote enthusiastically about it in her *Prospect of Western Travel,* believing that it was the first Christmas tree set up in America. However, as we have already observed, the custom was started earlier in Pennsylvania.

Mrs. Follen's account is a charming picture of an early Christmas party in America. "Every Christmas since Charles was two years old, his father

KRISS KRINGLE'S CHRISTMAS TREE

E. FERRETT & CO.

PHILADELPHIA

1845.

Title page from *Kriss Kringle's Christmas Tree*. Dr. Alfred L. Shoemaker described this volume as "the most important Christmas book in the United States." (Library of Congress photo)

Popcorn and cranberries strung together, gingerbread men, candles in holders, cookies, candy canes, baubles, horns of candy and heirloom ornaments add a nostalgic touch to this table tree by Mrs. T. Stacey Bubier and Mrs. C. Heywood Green

had dressed a Christmas-tree for him, after the fashion of his own country. This was always the happiest day in the year to him. He spared no pains, no time, in adorning the tree, and making it as beautiful as possible . . .

"Every one in the family contributed to its decoration. Then he placed wax tapers on every branch, carefully, so as to light the tree perfectly, but not to set fire to anything. All the children of our acquaintance were invited to see it; after tea, at the ringing of a bell, the door of the room where the tree was placed was opened, and the children entered. Dr. Follen always placed himself where he could see the children's faces as they entered. 'It was in their eyes,' he used to say, 'that he loved best to see the Christmas-tree.' After the lights were burned out, and the baskets of sugarplums that hung on the tree were distributed, the children danced or played games the rest of the evening."

Miss Martineau was equally expressive and enthusiastic as she recorded her impressions of that unforgettable evening. "I was present at the introduction into the new country of the spectacle of the German Christmas-tree. My little friend Charley and three companions had been long preparing for this pretty show. The cook had broken her eggs carefully in the middle for some weeks past, that Charley might have the shells for cups; and these cups were gilded and coloured very prettily . . . We were all engaged in sticking on the last of the seven dozen of wax-tapers, and in filling the gilded egg-cups and gay paper cornucopiae with comfits, lozenges, and barley-sugar. The tree was the top of a young fir, planted in a tub, which was ornamented with moss. Smart dolls and other whimsies glittered in the evergreen, and there was not a twig which had not something sparkling upon it . . .

"It really looked beautiful; the room seemed in a blaze, and the ornaments were so well hung on that no accident happened, except that one doll's petticoat caught fire. There was a sponge tied to the end of a stick to put out any supernumerary blaze, and no harm ensued. I mounted the steps behind the tree to see the effect of opening the doors. It was delightful. The children poured in, but in a moment every voice was hushed. Their faces were upturned to the blaze, all eyes wide open, all lips parted, all steps arrested. Nobody spoke, only Charley leaped for joy. The first symptom of recovery was the children's wandering round the tree. At last a quick pair of eyes discovered that it bore something eatable, and from that moment the babble began again . . . I have little doubt the Christmas-tree will become one of the most flourishing exotics of New-England."

Within a few years this story was retold in a penny pamphlet published by the American Sunday School Union at Boston and the idea spread rapidly to all parts of New England and beyond its borders.

In 1833, along the Mississippi in St. Clair County, Illinois, there were no fir trees for decking out at Christmas. Yet this fact did not deter Gustave Koerner and his neighbors from contriving a tree of their own making. They

used a "small green-barked sassafras tree," and decorated it with apples, bits of ribbon and bright paper, polished red haws (the fruit of the hawthorn tree) and glossy hazel and hickory nuts. Koerner made mention of all sorts of sweets which "Aunt Caroline used to make so excellently." They added candles too, as the account goes, and together with their German friends observed Christmas around this makeshift tree. It served as a vivid reminder of the homeland which helped them to recall the friends and relatives they had left behind, and the day came to a close in an atmosphere that was both nostalgic and melancholy. In the Krausnick memoirs there is a touching description of the first family tree set up in Cincinnati, Ohio, in 1835.

Like Charles Follen who found Boston a haven from the political upheavals occurring in Germany in the 1820's, another young German scholar, one Charles F. E. Minnegerode, made Christmas tree fame in Williamsburg, Virginia. Arrested for his political affiliations while a student at the University of Geissen, this young man who hailed from Hesse-Darmstadt, the region from which the Hessians of Revolutionary fame had come, spent many months in prison. His only reading material was his Bible.

In 1842 he obtained a position teaching Greek and Latin at the College of William and Mary. He became friendly with Judge Nathaniel B. Tucker and his family. That very Christmas he went to the nearby woodland and obtained an evergreen and brought it to the Tucker house where he set it up and decorated it. Since there were no ornaments available for this strange creation, he used popcorn, nuts, colored paper, and made his own decorations. A member of the family recalled that he improvised wire to fasten the candles to the tree and placed the traditional gold star at the top.

News of the tree spread and soon all the neighbors wanted to bring their children. There was carol singing and there were German games which the young professor (known to them affectionately as Minck) taught the children. From this modest beginning, the tradition grew over the years. Dr. Janet Kimbrough, a descendant of Judge Tucker, recalls that great care was taken to prevent danger from fire. The men of the family and other male guests lit the candles with long sticks. One end was used for lighting, and there was a sponge attached to the other end to put out any blaze that might occur. From this tree developed the custom of lighting a community tree each year, which is set up near the Tucker residence on Christmas Eve in the town of Williamsburg.

Another early record of interest in Virginia is the tree which August Bodeker set up in his store in Richmond in 1846 to the amazement and joy of his friends and neighbors.

A newspaper account from Rochester, New York, December 23, 1840, entitled "Germany in America!" tells of the forthcoming celebration that the German Protestant children will participate in at their Meeting House, and that American children are invited to attend this "custom of the Old Country" on Christmas Eve. A few years later another Lutheran church in the city staged a tree with "a magical representation of the Nativity of Christ, the mountains of Judah and the plains of Bethlehem."

A painting of Martin Luther's family gathered around a lighted Christmas tree — the work of Carl August Schwerdgeburth, 1845 — which was reproduced in many Pennsylvania church periodicals, contributed greatly in popularizing the tree. Ten years later a book entitled *Luther's Christmas Tree* by T. Stork had wide distribution in Sunday Schools. This little publication and other pamphlets issued by various denominations gave real impetus to the new Christmas symbol.

A handsomely decorated commemorative plate memorializes a German tailor who set up and decorated the first Christmas tree in Wooster, Ohio, in 1847. August Imgard came to the community as a young man and made history by establishing a beloved custom of his homeland. The tree, obtained with great effort, was set up for his nephews and nieces and proved to be an immediate sensation. The metal star which he made with the aid of a local tinsmith is now a cherished family heirloom. With the same warm spirit that inspired the townspeople to adopt his idea more than a century ago, the name of August Imgard is kept green even to this day with a tree which is placed at the entrance to his tomb each year at Christmas.

Cleveland, Ohio, has its tale about the tree too, which Hertha Pauli has told in a most enchanting manner in *The Story of the Christmas Trees*. Rev. Henry Schwan placed a Christmas tree in his church in 1851 and received strong opposition from some of the townspeople who looked upon the practice as the revival of a pagan custom. In fact, he was admonished to the point of threats, but after looking into the background and historical significance of the tree, he was able to persuade them that it was truly a Christian custom.

The reaction to the early use of the tree in Philadelphia, in Boston, in Williamsburg, and other communities had been one of curious delight in a quaint German custom. It was something to amuse the children. But a tree lighted with candles, placed in a church, was something quite different. Perhaps, had it been set up for the Sunday School, the event might have attracted little or no attention.

All too little known is the story of two Christmas trees set up in Charleston, South Carolina, for the Swedish nightingale, Miss Jenny Lind, for Christmas, 1850. She had come to America for a concert tour at the invitation of the fabulous P. T. Barnum. Everywhere she appeared, she was received with great acclaim and was handsomely rewarded for her efforts. Her arrival in Charleston is reported in the *Courier*: "As she landed, hundreds of enthusiastic citizens

Phineas T Barnum

Jenny Lind

jammed sidewalks and streets to see her ushered triumphantly to the Charleston Hotel where the ladies of the town had erected a brilliant Christmas tree in front of her window." Much of the money she made was distributed to charities here and in her homeland. Despite her success and the glamour which attended it, Jenny Lind was deeply attached to the traditions and customs she had known at home. Of all seasons of the year, she had an abiding love for Christmas, the home feast with its tree and all the attendant merriment. Accordingly, as Barnum relates in his autobiography: "Christmas was at hand, and Jenny determined to honor it in the way she had often done in Sweden. She had a beautiful Christmas tree privately prepared, and from its boughs depended a variety of presents for members of the company. These gifts were encased in paper, with the name of the recipients written on each.

"After spending a pleasant evening in her drawing-room, she invited us into the parlor, where the 'surprise' awaited us. Each person commenced opening the packages bearing his or her address, and although every individual had one or more pretty presents, she had prepared a joke for each. Mr. Benedict, for instance, took off wrapper after wrapper from one of his packages, which at first was as large as his head, but after having removed some forty coverings of paper, it was reduced to a size smaller than his hand, and the removal of the last envelope exposed to view a piece of cavendish tobacco. One of *my* presents, choicely wrapped in a dozen coverings, was a jolly young Bacchus in Parian marble—intended as a pleasant hit at my temperance principles!"

By 1850, the Christmas tree had become the height of fashion for the festive season. Sarah Hale, editor of *Godey's Lady's Book* "borrowed" the picture of the "Christmas Tree at Windsor Castle" which had appeared in the *Illustrated London News* Christmas Supplement of 1848 and used it in her December issue. She used the picture again in 1860. Curiously enough, in featuring the tree in her select publication, Mrs. Hale made some slight changes in the original engraving by removing Queen Victoria's coronet as well as Albert's mustache, his sash and the royal insignia that hung round his neck. The "pretty German toy" which Prince Albert set up for the delight of his children received the stamp of approval from one of America's leading arbiters of fashion.

Surely Sarah Hale must have known that the custom had been fairly well established in many Pennsylvania communities several decades before Prince Albert launched the tree so ceremoniously in England. But the fact that a new fashion had a royal flourish gave it the prestige so necessary in those days to its success and popularity. In 1852, the editor of *Gleason's Pictorial Drawing Room Companion* declared, "Already is the Christmas tree established as one of the household gods of New England and a large portion of the states."

The beginning of the Christmas tree trade in New York City is due to Mark Carr, a woodman of the lower Catskills, who, having read of celebrations in the city where boughs and wreaths played an important part in the decorations, conceived the idea in 1851. The stately young firs growing about his modest mountain home might possibly be turned to some account, at a season when he had little else to do. In any case, the chopping and transportation would comprise the whole cost of the enterprise. He broached the subject to his family; but his wife laughed at it. "Who would spend their money for green truck which could be had for the cutting?" The sons, however, sided with their father, and offered to help.

One fine day in mid-December two ox-sleds were laden with thrifty young conifers and driven over the rough roads, through the deep snow to the river at Catskill village. Mr. Carr then proceeded with them to New York. For one old-fashioned silver dollar, he secured a small strip of sidewalk on the corner of Greenwich and Vesey Streets, and there he set forth his woodland wares.

Quick and certain was his success, exceeding his fondest expectations. Eagerly customers flocked to purchase the fragrant mountain novelties, at what appeared to the unsophisticated countryman exorbitant prices. It did not take long to exhaust the entire stock. Then, highly elated, Mark enjoyed a few days of city life before returning home to gladden the hearts of his boys with the result of their venture, and, it may be, to crow a little over Dame Carr. The following season he brought down a far larger load. Thus started the evergreen trade which has increased to such vast proportions that by 1890 the hills of Rip Van Winkle alone furnished annually two hundred thousand trees. Mark Carr's old corner commanded a rental of one hundred dollars, instead of one hundred cents, for the week or two preceding Christmas.

From the period 1850 on, there are stories galore in magazines and newspapers describing wonderful trees and truly magical Christmas yards. Adjectives like "wonderful" and "magical" seem truly appropriate, for such they were to all who beheld them. Then, too, the word wonderful has strong significance among the Pennsylvania Germans who have used it with feeling and subtle expression over the years. When they say something is "wonderful good" they mean it and it truly is.

The observance of Christmas at the White House, or the President's House, as it was known then, had an auspicious beginning, since George and Martha Washington loved this season of the year. With the first Christmas reception in Philadelphia, they established a precedent which was to set the tempo and spirit of this important observance in the years that followed. As members of the Episcopal Church, they celebrated the feast of Christmas with ceremony and jollity. Although the Washingtons did not have a tree, they greatly enjoyed the festivities and especially the family party with their grandchildren.

In later years, Washington turned his attention to the collecting and growing of holly trees on the grounds at Mount Vernon. In those days, everyone who decorated homes and churches for Christmas used our native American

holly which was plentiful. It had been known to the English settlers by many names, among them Christmas, Christmas Tree, and Prickly Christmas. In addition to its decorative use for the holidays and its welcome appearance in the winter landscape, Washington admired the holly as an outstanding native tree worthy of cultivation. Today homeowners all over America are planting this tree of Christmas in their gardens. Without being aware of the significance of his hobby, General Washington set the stage for a far-reaching tradition.

A full report of Christmas with the Presidents from Washington's time to the present has no place in this account of the Christmas tree story, but it is nonetheless an engaging, fascinating, and colorful chapter in our social history.

Andrew Jackson added gusto to the life of Washington society in his day, and he reveled in Christmas. His French chef was famous for frozen ices which were the wonder and envy of the Capital city. In addition to those formed in the shape of familiar fruits there was "a small frosted pine tree with toy animals around it" to delight young and old who attended the President's party in 1835.

Franklin Pierce, a native of New Hampshire, introduced the Christmas tree to the White House during his time of office in the year 1856. When we realize that the Sunday School movement had begun to popularize the idea in Boston, New York, and Philadelphia through the publication of pamphlets describing Charles Follen's tree set up in 1832 in Boston and other trees used at church and Sunday School gatherings, it is not surprising that President Pierce's guests were members of the New York Avenue Presbyterian Church.

Several decades later Benjamin Harrison, who came to the White House in 1889, made a warmhearted observance of Christmas which he considered "the most sacred religious festival of the year." He expressed himself with enthusiasm and deep feeling that folk had a "duty — as Christians to make merry" and told of the "old-fashioned" Christmas tree which his family would have. It doesn't take long for a new custom or tradition that becomes generally accepted and popular to receive the name "old-fashioned."

The vigorous Theodore Roosevelt has given us several bits of Christmas tree history which add color and zest to the ever-growing story of the tree in America. An ardent conservationist, he became alarmed at the ever-increasing demand for evergreen trees and felt that this custom would eventually deplete our great forests, which even then were showing the ravages of thoughtless cutting. In fact, his convictions were so strong that he forbade the use of a Christmas tree in his house. He was red-faced indeed when he learned that his sons Archie and Quentin had smuggled a tree into the closet of Archie's room. His reprimand sent them to call on Gifford Pinchot, the leading conservationist of his day and a close friend of the President, in whose cabinet he served. Pinchot assured Roosevelt that if properly handled the cutting of

Victorian Christmas card about 1870. Draw string makes branches of tree move. Essex Institute Collection

An illustration from Frank Leslie's *Popular Monthly*, December 1890

Christmas trees could be an asset to timberlands. The outcome of the story is told in a letter which the President wrote to Master James Garfield, the day after Christmas in 1902.

"Jimmikins:

"Yesterday morning at a quarter of seven all the children were up and dressed and began to hammer at the door of their mother's and my room, in which their six stockings, all bulging out with queer angles and rotundities, were hanging from the fireplace. So their mother and I got up, shut the window, lit the fire, taking down the stockings, of course, put on our wrappers and prepared to admit the children. But first there was a surprise for me, also for their good mother, for Archie had a little Christmas tree of his own which he had rigged up with the help of one of the carpenters in a big closet; and we all had to look at the tree and each of us got a present off of it. There was also one present each for Jack the dog, Tom Quartz the kitten, and Algonquin the pony, whom Archie would no more think of neglecting than I would neglect his brothers and sisters."

Theodore Roosevelt will long be remembered for many things, and not the least of these is the teddy bear, named for him, which first appeared under American Christmas trees more than half a century ago. No other President's name could have been more happily kept alive through a toy than this man's who loved children tenderly.

A New York importer, on a trip to Germany, paid a visit to Frau Margarette Steiff of Gingen, Wurtemburg, a bedridden invalid who made stuffed toys for her own children and a few to sell. In discussing toys with her, he showed her a cartoon from a Washington newspaper featuring one of Teddy Roosevelt's recent bear hunts. Amused and inspired by the picture of the colorful Roosevelt standing over a small bear he had shot, Frau Steiff immediately created a jointed, stuffed toy, which she called a "Teddy Bear." When it was offered at the Leipzig Toy Fair in 1903, it topped every toy in sales, and within three years was a leading item on toy counters throughout the world. Here was a boy's doll and one that girls liked, too. In the years since, many similar jointed, stuffed figures of the teddy bear type have been created and today they number in the millions in America alone. Over a twenty-five year period following World War I, one toy firm alone produced four million teddy bears.

The names of Calvin and Grace Coolidge are linked with the lighting of the first national Christmas tree, a gigantic spruce from Coolidge's native Vermont hills, which was placed on the White House lawn in 1923. The following year he officiated at a cermony in Washington sponsored by the American Forestry Association to champion the use of living Christmas trees throughout the country. Since that time, the annual ceremony has become a vital and colorful part of the Christmas observances at the Capitol.

Perhaps nowhere in America can be found more fascinating settings for the Christmas tree than in Pennsylvania, where the "putz" or Christmas yard is staged annually as a part of the home celebration. Folk of Pennsylvania German ancestry have carried the custom to various parts of the country during the past century so that the custom is becoming more widely known. But among the Moravians and their descendants one finds some of the finest examples even today.

The word putz, derived from the old German word *putzen* means "to adorn, to decorate, to dress up, to put in order, or to clean and polish." Thus the name, as used for more than a hundred years in this region, connotes a very special but widely varied landscape "built under and around the Christmas tree," portraying the birth of Christ in superb detail. There seems to be no limit to the number of features included, and sometimes there is a kind of incongruity in the settings which literally teem with figures, landscape features, villages, churches, castles, lights which have largely replaced the candles of earlier days, cookies, fruit, the whole sometimes complete with a starry sky.

Quantities of moss are used to mold the landscape setting and an immense amount of work displaying surprising creative skill and ingenuity are employed in making a putz. It can vary in size from a table setting to an entire room, limited only by the area available. The finished creation is one of pure fancy and delight inspired by great reverence. With such a setting for the Christmas tree how could anyone possibly fail to grasp its meaning!

There was a "village with its church and rows of stiff poplar trees; the pleasant minglings of bird and beast and fish, all in perfect peace with one another, as became them at Christmas time; the stable where the 'blessed child' was born; the mill hoisting up its bags and letting them down again, as long as the hidden machinery remained in working order, whilst the miller smoked his pipe, and his dog kept up a very energetic, if somewhat methodical jumping at his feet; all these, and a thousand other recollections, rise before the memory, and force us to the conclusion that putzes are a great institution, and ought not to be allowed to die out." (*The Moravian,* December, 1867.)

All kinds of wonderful creations were developed for use in the Christmas landscape scenes. There were revolving trees, mechanized scenes, and moving figures. Pyramids with elaborate tops like those of a many-armed windmill were among the novelties. Whenever the ingenious German mind dreamed up something, it was worth a second look and was all the more fascinating in a Christmas yard.

CHAPTER VIII

The Tree in Other Countries

SETTING UP the Christmas sheaves for the birds is one of those customs filled with mystic meaning that lends great charm to the holiday season in the Scandinavian countries. Linked with this age-old practice of providing a Christmas tree for the birds is an equally ancient belief. To early man, every bit of food consumed was full of nourishment, but the last bite was what counted. From this notion developed the custom of making a figurine from the last grain harvested in the fields. The image was placed beside the head of the house at the Christmas table and given brandy and the choicest of food. Then it was set out on the housetop or the barn. If the birds ate all the grain, the omen indicated a good harvest the following year.

Sheaves or stooks of grain, securely tied, were placed on long poles made of pine or spruce, and stuck into the ground, often near a gate or nailed to the peak of the barn roof. This notion has found warm acceptance in America among Audubon Societies and bird clubs, and every gardener worth his salt makes an effort to provide either a tree or a feeding station for our feathered friends during the winter. Christmas is a most auspicious time, especially since discarded holiday trees can be utilized in this manner. Originally a country custom in the Scandinavian countries, it soon spread to the city. These tillers of the soil knew and loved the old Christmas legends about the animals and this provision for the birds is but one expression of it.

The practice was known in the city of Stockholm as early as the middle of the seventeenth century. As the custom became more widespread, the poles with their green tops intact were decked with garlands in a variety of ways. Sometimes they were fashioned in the form of crosses, hence the name Christmas Cross. The idea of a Christmas tree for birds has become increasingly popular in Sweden and throughout the Scandinavian countries. Visitors tell of the delightful custom so evident in the cities there today in which evergreens are placed on terraces and in gardens, laden with suet, seed, and other favorite forms of bird food.

Helge Akerhielm, in discussing Christmas in Sweden, associates the Christmas tree with the Tree of Life which was linked with the ancient ancestral tree to be found on every farm in bygone days. "The growth and well-being

of all that grew on the farm were dependent upon the growth and well-being of the tree . . . Not infrequently, the ancestral tree was the home of the farmer's brownie." This is actually the Yule tree of the farm yard, which was also popular in Germany.

Although the Christmas tree did not become widely known in Sweden until the second half of the nineteenth century, there are records of a tree in a castle in Soderman and one as early as 1741, and a colorful account of one at Stockholm in 1821. However, once introduced it became popular there and in all the other Scandinavian countries, as it did in England and America. In Sweden, it is not considered good taste to overdecorate the tree. As in other

A Christmas tree for the birds is traditional in Scandinavian countries

countries, the children look forward to the days after Christmas when it can be plundered before it is taken down.

Jenny Lind, who brought fame to her native Sweden in the middle of the nineteenth century, had such devotion to her tree that whenever she was away from home at Christmas, she celebrated with a tree. In a memoir by H. S. Holland and W. S. Rockstro we read: "Her Christmas-tree! That was what she could never miss: all through her life, she loved, like a child, the home-feast, the children's fun of Christmastide. Those who knew her can recall no scene to which she could more deliciously abandon herself with brimming joy than a children's dance at Christmas. All the old Swedish merriment and motion would bubble up in her at such a time: and her face would laugh all over with exuberant humour, and her whole body seemed to dance. She had a gaiety that was infectious: and no wonder that she managed to make even a Lübeck hotel merry with her radiance." A few years later, Miss Lind made newspaper headlines with her tree in America.

Then there is the heart-warming account by Hans Christian Andersen, the beloved Norwegian story teller and writer, of a Christmas spent in Berlin in 1845. Jenny Lind was there too. When she learned that he too was spending Christmas away from home she planned a party for her "brother," for this was her manner of addressing him in accordance with old-world Scandinavian usage. Speaking of his Christmas festival in his autobiography, he wrote: "Amidst all this festive excitement, this amiable and zealous interest in my behalf, one evening, and one only, was unoccupied, on which I suddenly felt the power of loneliness, in its most oppressive form—Christmas Eve, the exact evening on which I always feel most festive, feel so glad to stand beside a Christmas-tree, enjoy so much the happiness of the children, and love to see the elders become children again. I heard afterwards that, in each one of the family circles in which I had truly been received as a relative, it had been supposed that I was already engaged elsewhere: but, in reality, I sat quite alone in my window and looked up at the star-bespangled heavens. That was the Christmas-tree that had been lighted up for me. 'Father in heaven!' I prayed, as the children pray, 'what wilt Thou give me?'

"When my friends heard of my lonely Christmas feast, they lighted up many Christmas-trees for me on the following evenings, and on the last evening in the year a little tree, with lights and pretty presents, was prepared for me alone—and that by Jenny Lind. The entire circle comprised herself, her companion and me. We three children of the North met together, on that Sylvester-evening, and I was the child for whom the Christmas-tree had been lighted up. With sisterly feeling, she rejoiced over my success in Berlin, and I felt almost vain of the sympathy of so pure, so womanly a being. Her praises were sounded everywhere, the praises, not of the artist only but of the woman. The two united awoke for her a true enthusiasm."

If Hans Christian Andersen had left us nothing more than this touching record of that memorable evening, the annals of the Christmas tree in Norway would be forever green. But his story, *The Fir Tree,* which has delighted millions of readers for a century or more, has made him an immortal chronicler of the emblem of Christmas.

The tree was introduced to France by Duchess Hélène of Orleans who brought it to the Tuileries in 1840. The Empress Eugénie enjoyed the new custom, but at first many of the middle class looked upon the tree as an intruder from Alsace. Twenty years later evergreen trees for Christmas were still not easy to obtain, but after the German Army had celebrated Christmas at Notre Dame Cathedral in 1870, the custom of the Christmas tree became more widespread.

Girls dance under the *May* at New Year's in Alsace

Christmas comes to the children of Alsace (Gustave Doré)

In France as in Italy and Spain and Portugal, the Christmas celebration for the children had long centered around the crib with all its figures. In many instances elaborate landscape settings were developed around the manger setting. Sometimes small trees, bits of moss, tiny plants, and other natural features were introduced. Since the crib held so strong a place in their hearts, and evergreens were not as plentiful as they were in Germany and the coun-

tries to the North, it is easy to understand why this import from Germany did not become deeply rooted. To be sure, the Italians cherished their pyramid decked with candles and greens which they called a *ceppo*.

In Austria, Switzerland, Poland, Holland, and other countries associated with German culture, the brightly bedecked tree made its way. In the various countries where the tree was introduced, it acquired individuality by way of the decorations used or added to the traditional apples, baubles, cookies, sweets, and candles.

In Alsace, it was the custom to set up a *may* in the public square for New Year's Day. A quick glance at old prints illustrating this decorated evergreen might bring to mind the thought that this custom was the forerunner of our community Christmas tree. Usually, the tree, its lower limbs stripped, was erected near a fountain. The name *may* does not relate to the month of the calendar year but means to decorate or to adorn. Ribbons, eggshells, dolls, and usually a figure of a shepherd or a man beating his wife were hung on the tree. The tree was put in place on New Year's Eve. The following day the girls of the village who set it up gathered for a dance and the boys were allowed to take part only when the girls granted permission. Curiously enough, this tree was allowed to remain standing throughout the year as a symbol of protection for the maidens who put it there. Parallel traditions of a similar kind are to be found in other countries.

On the Island of Chios, tenants greeted their landlords on Christmas morning with a type of man-made tree called a *rhamna*. It was a pole decked with wreaths and garlands of myrtle, olive, and orange leaves. Such flowers as geraniums, anemones, together with oranges, lemons, and colored paper were added for color. This old custom may have had its origin in the ancient Greek portable Maypole known as an *Eiresione*. This was a branch hung with "wool, acorns, figs, cakes, fruits of all sorts and sometimes wine jars."

Among the Circassians a century ago, it was the fashion to bring a young pear tree into the house at an autumn festival. The ceremony was carried out with music and song. Ornamented with candles, the tree had a cheese as a crowning decoration and around it the family made merry. Later it was taken to the courtyard for the remainder of the year.

In Japan, toys are used at New Year's to decorate branches of trees and, after being carried about to the delight of the children, they are distributed among them. Thus, the introduction of the Christmas tree by American missionaries was a custom which charmed them without seeming strange. The Chinese call Christmas the Festival of the Holy Birth, and the tree is known there as the Tree of Light. There is no problem in choosing decorations for trees in these countries where some of the greatest expressions of art are evolved from paper.

The Japanese custom of hanging toys on trees at New Year's

The observance of Christmas in the tropics around the world, as well as in Australia and New Zealand, is kept traditional by the use of greens native to the various countries, and other colorful decorations of local origin. During the past century many kinds of trees have been adapted to take the place of the fir of northern latitudes. The tradition of the Christmas tree has left a deep imprint and is not likely to be forgotten, for its roots reach to the heart.

The decorations tell a story. (Courtesy, Lauren Ford)

CHAPTER IX

The Light of the World

"WHAT a strange thing a light is, I thought. It burns and glows by offering itself, I thought. And thought that this, too, was a strange thought, yet so right. So natural, as if life were like that too, like the light." Symbols are not always easy to explain in words, but a Swedish soldier of World War II who wrote a letter home knew what a symbol was. He had received a Christmas candle from his mother and lighted it in his lonely barracks on Christmas Eve as was the custom he had known at home. In the opening chapter of *Swedish Christmas*, Gunnar Edman has expressed its meaning vividly: "The flame — the most universal of all symbols — burns and illuminates by offering itself."

Thus, a candle or any kind of a light when lit becomes a sermon and the meaning of "I am the Light of the World. I am the Resurrection and the Life" shines forth in all its clarity. Yes, and this is the thought that often stirs unconsciously in the heart of many a Christmas shopper even though the merchant who set up the brightly lighted tree had his thoughts on the cash register. The bright lights of Christmas which glow each year in every community in America and reach to the ever-closer corners of the globe have not lost their meaning, for it is beyond price. Symbols are understood only in the language of the heart. What a strange thing light is!

The ancient Hebrew festival known as *Chanukkah* was called the "Feast of Lights." It occurred in the ninth month of the Jewish calendar, which corresponds to our Christmas season, and was a most colorful ceremony to commemorate the rededication of the Temple. Quantities of candles and lamps were used to light the temple as well as the traditional seven-branch candelabra which added to the brilliance and beauty of the occasion. Since we know that the early Christians were steeped in the Hebraic tradition, we can well understand how meaningful lights were on festive occasions.

It is from this ancient origin that the Christian symbolism of the lighted candle has come. During the Middle Ages, a large candle lit on Christmas Eve at church service and also at home served as a reminder of the Star of Bethlehem, or "as a Light to lighten the Gentiles." From this practice came the widespread use of candles such as the Lightstock or pyramid described in

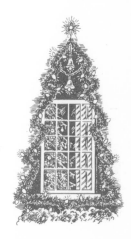

Chapter Four. Thus, when lights were transferred to the Christmas tree, the tradition became even more widespread and significant.

The story connecting the origin of the lighted Christmas tree with Martin Luther relates that he lighted a tree with candles to suggest to his children how the stars that lighted the heavens shone on the earth the night that Christ was born, and every Christmas thereafter.

In an old French epic of the thirteenth century, *Durmars le galois,* we read a descripion of "a tree whose branches are covered from top to bottom with lit candles, of which some stand properly and some upside down. But still more shining than these, a resplendent Child is sitting on top. Terrified and wondering what this means, Durmars asks the Pope, and receives the answer: 'The lit tree is humanity, the upright lights are the good men, the reversed lights the bad men, the Child is the Saviour.' "

Various omens were associated with candles according to the way in which they were lighted, or how well the light burned. In Scotland, before the Reformation, it was believed that if the candle went out before midnight evil would befall the family. If it continued to burn, it was extinguished after midnight and kept for use at the death watch of the head of the house. In the British Isles it was customary for candlemakers to give large candles to their customers at Christmas, and the custom was carried on in this country until local grocery and provision stores were replaced by supermarkets. In Ireland a large candle is always placed in the window on Christmas Eve to show the way and give a sign of welcome to the Holy Family. In the Slavic countries, the candle used is one blessed by the priest.

In the Scandinavian countries two candles are placed on the festive board. One represents the husband, the other the wife. It is believed that the candle which burns out last foretells the survivor of the wedded pair. A three-branched candle representing the Trinity is also used at Christmas in many parts of Europe. In pre-Christian times, the salutation for the winter solstice was, "I give you light for the year." After Bethlehem the message became, "I give you Christ — the Light of the World."

The subtle beauty and atmospheric quality of candlelight, especially on an evergreen, has long been a source of joy to all beholders. Yet the danger element when lighted candles are placed on a partially dry evergreen has always been a serious problem. Thus, the Christmas trees of bygone days were lighted for a brief time only, and carefully watched. It was an event upon which all the family gathered to see the glow of dozens of candles, and they were blown out within a matter of minutes as the melted wax dripped on the spreading branches. There are stories galore of sticks with sponges and buckets of water kept on hand as fire precautions, and there are accounts of tragedies resulting from candlelit trees.

Painting of Martin Luther's tree

Victorian tree

Four Christmas trees

Christmas tree at Strassburg

During the Victorian era, Christmas lights made of colored glass, hung with loops of wire, came into fashion for use on Christmas trees. They were safer than candles set in metal holders clipped to the branches, and gave a pleasing light because of the rich coloring of the glass. Hand-blown types of such decorative lights were made in America before the Revolution by Baron Steigel and Caspar Wistar and were referred to as Christmas lights. These lamps had floating wicks and burned oil which floated on water. Candles were also used in them. Patterned glass, like thousand-eye and diamond-cut, were particularly popular because of the sparkling light they reflected. Undoubtedly, the early glassmakers brought the idea from Europe, for these lamps were popular there for outdoor ceremonies at various seasons of the year. When Jenny Lind visited Charleston in 1850, the ladies of the city used quantities of these lamps to light a Christmas tree outside her hotel window.

Gas jets for lighting were used a hundred years ago. The Pittsburgh *Missionary Magazine* describes an elaborate Christmas tree set up in a New York City church on which "nearly two hundred jets sparkled and glimmered through the branches." In the decades that followed, other newspaper accounts told of trees similarly lighted, sometimes for public display.

The use of electric light bulbs on trees was a novelty in the 1880's, but it was not long before colored lights became the vogue for indoor and outdoor use. About 1895 Ralph E. Morris, an employee of the New England Telephone and Telegraph Company, obtained some twelve-volt flashlight size bulbs made for telephone switchboards and fashioned them into a string of lights for his family tree. He may not have been the first individual to use miniature electric lights on a Christmas tree, but his ingenuity was typical of efforts to develop safe lighting for indoor use.

The advent of modern lighting brought new glamour and glory to the old-fashioned Christmas tree. It could be illuminated safely indoors or out and today it provides one of our principal sources of municipal decoration in cities and towns all over America. Every kind of tree, including evergreens, shade trees, and shrubs of all sizes and types, provides a setting for electric lights. When overdone the effect can be garish and it sometimes is, but with well-planned dramatic lighting, particularly when spotlights are used, the result has made Christmas a memorable spectacle for young and old in every village and town across the land. In fact, America has earned the reputation for creating the most elaborate Christmas displays to be seen anywhere in the world.

Public-spirited citizens working with town officials have encouraged a spirit of friendly rivalry among communities. Even before lighting was attempted on this level, it had been widely developed in neighborhoods, particularly in the years following World War I. As a result, pilgrimages to see the lights

and other decorations have become commonplace as a part of our Christmas festivities. Like our ancestors, we all enjoy the gleaming lights that flash in the twilight and brighten the dark December nights.

Community-minded citizens throughout the nation have written a bright chapter in the history of Christmas in America. But, for the most part, their individual contributions are best known and appreciated by their friends and neighbors. Residents of Montana, who claim Eureka as the Christmas tree capital of America, point with pride to the fact that the "Christmas tree lady of the nation" resides in Butte. She is Alma Margaret Higgins, a diminutive white-haired woman who, for nearly forty years, has championed the cause of living Christmas trees throughout the country, and the annual lighting ceremonies connected with them.

In 1923, Mrs. Higgins wrote an article on her favorite subject for the December issue of *American Forests*. The following year, the American Forestry Association spearheaded a movement to stimulate interest in the planting of evergreen trees throughout the country. A tree was planted on the White House lawn and was lighted with colorful ceremony by President and Mrs. Calvin Coolidge, a custom which has been continued by Presidents Hoover, Roosevelt, Truman, and Eisenhower. Special observances have attended the lighting each year, including an annual message of peace and good will.

From the colorful ceremony at the White House, the idea spread and soon became popular among community groups, institutions of various kinds, and homeowners. Mrs. Higgins, spurred on by the enthusiastic support she received, was instrumental in spreading the idea through pamphlets, illustrated lectures, and photographic contests. Again in 1937, her message appeared in print in *American Forests*. Women's Clubs and civic organizations helped to further the idea by means of a Christmas Tree Questionnaire which Mrs. Higgins prepared. She wrote a pageant that made people everywhere aware of the Christmas tree. Her interest in conservation, her enthusiasm for the symbolic decorations of the tree, its legends, its traditions and history — in fact, every phase of the Christmas tree and its story, was projected as she championed the cause of living Christmas trees.

She knows her subject intimately and from every angle, and presents it at lectures with warm enthusiasm as she recalls story after story. One that she never tires of recounting was written by Valentine Williams, Captain of the Irish Guards, and published in the New York *Times*: "The greatest tribute to the Christmas spirit our age has ever known occurred during the World War in 1914, when gray figures from the German trenches came over to the English line with little Christmas trees, and cried in broken English, 'Merry Christmas, Tommy!' That Christmas Eve, lighted Christmas trees formed a chain of light all along the endless German line of communications from the front line in France to German headquarters. Before anybody realized what

was happening, men from the trenches on either side were scrambling into No-Man's Land, laughing, cheering, singing. Then rifles were laid aside, hands were clasped in Christmas friendship, cigars and cigarettes handed out and gifts exchanged. The Germans sang, *Stille Nacht, Heilige Nacht* and *O Tannenbaum,* and the English responded with 'Good King Wenceslas.'"

Alma Margaret Higgins stages numerous educational exhibits to show her enthusiasm for the traditions of the Christmas tree

Bringing Home Christmas from *Godey's Lady's Book*

CHAPTER X

A New Business Boom

GROWING AND SELLING Christmas trees is big business in America, representing nearly 50 million dollars annually. At present, more than 40 million trees are required each Christmas season to meet the demand, which has increased by more than twenty per cent in the past ten years. According to the United States Forest Service, 40,500,000 living trees were sold for Christmas, 1959. Of this number, nearly a third are imported from Canada. The major portion of our trees are grown in our northern states, either harvested from the wild or cut from commercial plantings. Montana, for example, produces nearly three million trees annually which are shipped to twenty-seven states and Cuba.

Surprisingly enough, more than 80 per cent of our Christmas trees are obtained from natural woodlands and pastures, while the remainder are raised on plantations or Christmas tree farms. More than 200,000 acres are devoted to production of this important crop, according to a recent report of the United States Department of Agriculture. Eastern red cedar, black spruce, several kinds of pine, white and red spruce, white fir, and Norway spruce, along with other miscellaneous needle evergreens, are also offered for sale annually.

An evergreen for indoor decoration is judged not only for its ability to hold its needles when cut, but also its general appearance, the strength of its branches, its color, fragrance, and the smoothness of its needles. For example, the prickly foliage of red cedar is a detriment in handling.

Throughout the eastern United States, the balsam fir is the best known and generally considered desirable. However, in those states to which the Douglas fir is shipped, it is equally popular. In the southeastern states the eastern red cedar and several kinds of pine are in demand. Sometimes the choice of a tree is based on sentimental association or local tradition, or it may depend on what is available from commercial plantings. Of this acreage, nearly half is located in New York state. The National Christmas Tree Growers Association co-ordinates the activities of growers in the various states.

As we look into the ever-increasing demand for Christmas trees, we must consider also the huge quantities of artificial trees of various kinds, numbering

Spruce Cones

Seeds in relation
to cones

Greatly enlarged
Pine seed

in the millions, which are sold annually. They vary in size from a few inches to six feet or more in height. Add to the forty million live trees, the wide variety of artificial types and those contrived from all sorts of materials by individuals, and the total number of trees used for decoration in America each Christmas season is colossal. Is it any wonder that this country is known as Christmas tree land?

Balsam fir used to top the list of favorite evergreens for Christmas tree use, but the Douglas fir, or Montana fir as it is known in the Christmas trade, stands in first place now, and represents 28 per cent of the annual sale.

Raising Christmas trees is a profitable business for farmers who have land of limited use in upland areas. Yet there is more to raising Christmas trees than merely taking a mattock, making a hole and inserting a tiny seedling. They require care, weeding, insect and disease control, and freedom from pests and animal damage.

It takes nine to ten years to raise a fir or spruce of good shape and size that will bring a fair price. Marketable pines can be produced in six or seven years. For the first few years, while seedlings are getting established, growth is slow, but by the end of the fourth year, growth becomes vigorous. Then the tree must be pruned or sheared at least once or twice in order to assure a shapely appearance. Christmas trees bring the best prices when they are of balanced pyramidal form and well branched on all sides. This means proper spacing when the trees are first set out, usually about six feet apart. Losses in seedling trees set out can range considerably, depending on weather, damage by animals, and the care that is given them.

From time to time we read of the practice of stump culture of Christmas trees. When trees fifteen to twenty-five years old are cut, allowing live branches to remain at the base, new buds develop on the stump. These adventitious buds, as they are called, form new leaders called "turn-ups" which develop into desirable trees in less time than it takes to grow a tree from seed.

There is more to harvesting Christmas trees than the mere cutting and shipping of which most of us think. Actually, the process involves several months and includes the selection of the trees, cutting, and removal to "a woods concentration yard" where they are sorted, graded, and sometimes tagged. Then they are bundled, butt-trimmed, hauled to a shipping center, and transported to market. E. M. Sowder, Extension Forester of the United States Department of Agriculture, gives us a vivid picture of the process which begins in October and sometimes earlier:

"A hatchet or pruning saw are the common tools used to cut the stems. Kept as moist as possible, the trees are carried or dragged by hand or occasionally hauled by horse or tractor to the concentration yard in the woods.

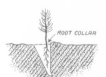

Planting

Place root collar
at ground level

Baling and tieing Christmas trees near Shelton, Washington. (U.S. Forest Service)

One man can cut and yard about two hundred trees per day. A wooden frame or rack is used to hold the trees while they are tied into bundles. Bundling makes trees easier to ship and prevents excessive drying. A bundle may have ten to twelve trees, four feet or so in size, or only one twelve-foot tree. While in the rack, the butt ends of the trees are trimmed for neat appearance and ease in handling. The trees must be hauled out before the depth of snow becomes an obstacle. Some Minnesota operators harvest trees nearly all year. This is made possible by placing the trees in cold storage soon after harvesting, cutting to size, and processing, which includes dipping in paint, drying the paint, trimming the butts, and packaging."

2" from plant
push dibble back
then forward to
firm soil

Sometimes we hear it said that the use of Christmas trees is a wanton waste of our natural resources which causes erosion of precious topsoil and upsets the balance of nature. These remarks are often made when surplus trees are observed in cities after the holidays. Balancing the supply on the national level is not easy. Producers are aware that the marketing of Christmas trees involves the same problems as those concerned with any semiperishable commodity. Actually, when we consider the millions of trees harvested annually, the surplus involved is not of great magnitude. Trees grown on comparatively poor soil develop more slowly than those in good soil, but they are usually of good quality in both form and foliage. Since evergreens are often the only suitable crop for some forest lands, they would be of little use if not cut and the owners would derive no other source of revenue from the land.

Foresters look upon the Christmas tree as a forest product that "probably yields as much joy and satisfaction to humanity" as any other produced by nature. Actually, with proper supervision, the cutting of Christmas trees

Fill and
pack firmly

benefits the remaining stand of growth. In some areas thinning is essential
to allow for the proper development of forest growth. Thus, sound conservation practices have produced an ever-growing phase of agriculture which is of
prime economic importance in our observance of Christmas.

Franklin Delano Roosevelt's name is strongly linked with the Christmas
tree tradition because he gained fame as a Christmas tree farmer at his place
in Hyde Park, New York. In fact, his keen interest in growing trees for
holiday use contributed greatly to the increase of small-scale plantings of
evergreens by owners of wood lots and pasture land not suited to other
commercial crops. Furthermore, the growing of Christmas trees as a hobby
by retired persons seeking a modest return on their investment as well as
pleasant and healthy recreation is another trend that has developed in the past
twenty years.

The Douglas fir, America's most popular evergreen in the Christmas tree
trade, is not a true fir. In fact, its identity was a source of confusion to
botanists for many years. Sir Archibald Menzies, a British botanist, discovered
it while exploring the region of Vancouver Island in 1791. To him, it was a
desirable evergreen but it had no name and he failed to give it one. It remained
for David Douglas, noted Scottish plant explorer, to make known this magnificent evergreen which now bears his name. He introduced it to England in
1827, where it became a much-admired ornamental evergreen.

From the beginning, this tree was a puzzle to the botanists who endeavored
to classify it. Eventually it was learned that there were only a few species in
the world, two in western North America and one in Japan. Strangely
enough, the tree which was named false hemlock, with yew-like needles
(*Pseudotsuga taxifolia*) was neither a yew nor a hemlock, nor was it a spruce
or a fir. Yet it had some of the distinguishing marks of all four evergreens.

To add to the confusion, the cones of Mr. Douglas's tree were different in
structure from any known kinds. They were oval, pendulous, soft cones with
strange little three-pronged flags thrusting from each of the scales. The
original scientific name has never been changed, but this mighty evergreen
is widely known as the Douglas tree, or Douglas fir.

In the Christmas trade, however, it is known as Montana fir, because three
million young trees are shipped out of that state each year for Christmas.
The blue-green needles are attached all around the upturned twigs and are
known to remain on the living tree from five to eight years. In addition to
its graceful upcurved growth, the tree when cut holds its needles from
St. Nicholas Day to Epiphany. This quality alone has given it top rank
among evergreens for use at Christmas. Then, too, Montana is exceedingly
proud of its reputation for quality in the production of Christmas trees, which
are grown, harvested, and refrigerated with great care.

Grading Christmas trees at Pike National Forest, Colorado. (U.S. Forest Service)

Cutting a white fir tree in Sierra National Forest. (U.S. Forest Service)

The Douglas fir is native to many parts of the Rocky Mountains, from British Columbia to the Mexican border. This majestic tree has been known to live for 750 years, ranks with the tallest in the world, and produces top-quality lumber.

The balsam fir, cherished as the most desirable of trees for Christmas in the eastern United States, is a particularly noteworthy evergreen because it retains its needles well when cut and gives off a delightful fragrance. These trees when mature reach sixty feet but when found at high altitudes are usually small shrubs. However, the trunk of a full-grown balsam fir may reach two feet in diameter. Commonly found in damp woods, and swamps, its native range extends from Newfoundland to Virginia, west to Iowa and north and west far into Canada. Although it is sometimes planted as an ornament in home gardens, it is not as successful as other species of firs.

Unlike most evergreens, the cones of the balsam fir are held erect and are highly decorative in various stages of development. The flat paper-like seeds shed from mature cones are quickly dispersed in the wind. It takes 43,800 seeds to produce a pound, and usually from 40 to 60 per cent of the seed can be expected to germinate. The wood is white and weak, soft and brittle, and of little value except for making crates and materials for packaging. Oil derived from this wood is commonly used to cement lenses together, to hold cover glasses on microscope slides, and for a variety of other purposes.

The fir tree is rich in legend and lore. Originally known as the fire tree, the most inflammable of woods, the fir was growing in England in Noah's time. John Gerarde, seventeenth century herbalist, tells us that after the flood subsided, the firs lay in the woods and marshy areas for centuries. Being full of resin, they burned like torches, hence the name firewood. In the north of Europe, the fir, like the pine, was king of the woodland. Consequently, the genie of the forest was always represented with an uprooted fir tree in his hand, and this tree was his favorite dwelling place. Old firs, like ancient oaks and birches, were especially revered when standing solitary.

In northern Germany newly married couples often carry lighted candles surrounded with branches of fir, perhaps in imitation of the Roman fasces. At Weimar it was the custom to plant fir trees in front of the homes of newly married couples. In Austrian Silesia the Maypole was always of fir. On midsummer night in the Harz mountains fir trees decorated with flowers and colored eggs were plunged into the ground before the festive dancing and singing took place. In northern Germany when the cattle were driven to pasture for the first time, it was the custom to decorate the last cow with small boughs of fir, expressing the wish that the pasturage be favorable to the fertility of the cattle. The balsam known as Balm of Gilead fir was the source of a very fine turpentine which was sometimes sold as the true Balm of Gilead.

CHAPTER XI

America Becomes Christmas Tree Land

VISITORS from other countries who come to our shores at Christmas are as dazzled by our observance of the season as are the millions of American children enjoying a Christmas tree for the first time. During the past half-century, the widespread use of community Christmas trees and the holiday lighting contests sponsored in neighborhoods have had a heartwarming influence. Few other communal efforts have done more to unify the various creeds and cultures within our borders. The tree stands as an emblem of hope and good will, harking back to its original significance.

Our European neighbors across the Atlantic have been aware of it almost since its inception in Pasadena, Philadelphia, Boston, New York, and other cities a half-century ago. Accordingly, when Norway wished to express its gratitude to England, a Christmas tree was sent in 1947 to be erected in London's Trafalgar Square. This gracious gesture did not go unnoticed and was widely publicized. It occurred at a season when men's hearts are warmer than usual and its effect was all the more meaningful.

In 1909, when the citizens of Pasadena, California, decorated a tree on Mount Wilson with electric lights, they laid the groundwork for a new custom in America.

New York City residents numbering twenty thousand or more gathered around "The Tree of Light" which was set up at Madison Square Park in 1912. Boston had an elaborate display of lights that year on its historic Common and this old city, like many another American community, has made a gala event of its public Christmas display ever since.

The next year the custom spread to Philadelphia where the great Norway spruce in Independence Square was proclaimed as "The Children's Christmas Tree." The Philadelphia *Record* on Christmas morning, 1913, gave this glowing account of the observance:

"High above the crowd came a flash of light from an unexpected place. It was the cupola of the tower of Independence Hall, the place where the Liberty Bell first rang out the news of the signing of the Declaration of

Independence. The oldest inhabitant at the Hall could not remember a time when the cupola had been lighted before. Into the lighted space stepped the six members of the celebrated trombone choir of the Moravian Church at Bethlehem, who welcome Christmas with the sounding of their trumpets every year in their home town. They had been brought to Philadelphia for the first time to take part in the city's first municipal celebration. Raising their long instruments to their lips, the trombonists sent forth a blast over the heads of the crowd. First they played 'How Brightly Shines the Morning Star,' then 'From Heaven High to Earth I Come,' and finally, very sweetly and in moderated tones, they sounded the notes of 'All My Heart This Night Rejoices.' "

Carols were sung at all these observances and, in the years that have followed, great significance has been added to these pleasant occasions with the setting up of large Christmas Cribs and life-size figures of the Nativity scene. Elaborate lighting effects as well as mechanized music have enhanced this kind of pageantry. Smaller communities like Salem, Oregon; Riverside, California; McDonald and Germantown in Pennsylvania; and Golden Gate Park in San Francisco had introduced the community tree by this time.

Wilmington, North Carolina, lays claim to the world's largest living Christmas tree, a 300-year-old live oak. More than 90 feet tall, with a trunk 14 feet in circumference, the spread of its branches extends well beyond a hundred feet. Appropriately enough, the tinsel on this great tree is Spanish moss, six tons of it. Elaborate ornaments and thousands of lights add to its decoration. This tree, growing in Hilton Park, provides a most appropriate setting for the singing of carols, the enacting of a Christmas play, as well as the setting for an elaborate crèche.

A giant sequoia known as the General Grant, more than 260 feet high, with its first limb breaking at half the tree's height from the ground, was selected as a living Christmas tree at King's Canyon National Park, California, in 1926. This ancient evergreen, believed to be more than 3,500 years old, was actually an old tree when Christ was born. Sanger, the nearest city, is the community responsible for the annual observance held there at high noon on Christmas day, when the voices of hundreds of carol singers are raised to proclaim the joy of the season.

Equally colorful is the story of a whole avenue of trees at Altadena, a suburb of Pasadena, California. Christmas Tree Lane, as it is known, consists of a great avenue of some two hundred cedars which Captain F. J. Woodbury planted on the grounds of his ranch before the turn of the century. He had seen these trees growing on the slopes of the Himalaya Mountains and, being greatly impressed with their beauty, brought seed back to California. The name deodar means "tree of God" and specimens in all stages of development are trees of great beauty. This planting now borders a public thoroughfare and the annual display of ten thousand lights arranged on the trees has attracted thousands of visitors annually.

Bethlehem, Pennsylvania, appropriately called the Christmas City of America, holds tenaciously to the traditions relating to its founding by a group of Moravian settlers more than two centuries ago. Here and in the town of Lititz, where Christmas pyramids were known before the Christmas tree was introduced, the sacred concept of Christmas has remained simple and traditional.

> Yet in the darkness shineth the everlasting Light;
> The hopes and fears of all the years are met in thee tonight.

Built around the cherished customs of the early settlers, a simple but impressive Christmas Eve Vigil is held in the Central Moravian Church. Elaborate preparations are made by the choirs, orchestra, trombonists, sacristans, and their assistants. Tasteful decorations focus attention on a life-size painting of the Nativity scene framed by the great arch behind the pulpit. Prior to Christmas, sacristans' helpers decorate thousands of beeswax candles, made locally, with gayly colored frills to give them a festive appearance and also to protect the hand from dripping wax.

The trombonists usher in the service with Christmas chorales, followed by the choir singing anthems. Some are by classic German composers, others by eighteenth century Moravian musicians. Then the choir and congregation join in the singing of many traditional hymns, including the chorale, "Not Jerusalem, Lowly Bethlehem," from which Bethlehem received its name.

Two parts of the service are awaited with particular eagerness by the children. One is the singing of the hymn, "Morning Star," in which the soloist is always a child whose selection has been kept a secret. The other is the moment during the latter half of the service when the sacristans appear with their trays of lighted candles. Each person is given one and the Vigil ends with congregation and choir singing by their friendly light. For the benefit of younger children there is a Love Feast in the afternoon. During the evening, families go visiting to see the putzes or Christmas landscapes which portray the nativity scene as associated with their own lives. On nearby South Mountain gleams the giant Electric Star of Bethlehem, and the center of this thriving city is bright with a lavish display of lights and gleaming Christmas trees.

The great plaza at Rockefeller Center in New York City has become world famous for its seasonal display of flowers, plants, and lighting effects. At Christmas it is especially memorable since the site adapts itself to unusually dramatic settings which are enjoyed by several million visitors each year. Not only the great tree itself but all the features that surround it create an illusion more wondrous than any fairy tale can convey. Exhibition skating, special ceremonies by church and youth groups, and the warmth and spirit generated

Avenue of Deodars, Altadena, California. Photo J. Allen Hawkins

by Christmas carols have been blended into a harmonious and truly beautiful pageant that perpetuates at least some of the spirit of bygone eras.

In Lake County, Florida, the palm is championed as the appropriate tree for Christmas and when lighted and decorated makes an unforgettable sight with its great spreading fronds making a broad pyramid. Chamber of Commerce leaders, spurred on by the Council of Federated Garden Clubs, have launched an intensive program for the use of various types and kinds of palms for indoor and outdoor use. Enthusiastic advocates point to the palms of the Holy Land as the inspiration for their idea, supported by the luxuriant specimens which grow in their state.

Tagging trees at Shelton, Washington. (U.S. Forest Service)

Some communities have gained fame for the size of the tree they decorate annually. In Pershing Square, Los Angeles, a white fir nearly a hundred feet tall was the source of great admiration, as was the 134-foot Douglas fir set up in Bellingham, Washington, the same year. It proved to be no small engineering feat to erect a 221-foot fir moved seventy miles into Northgate, a shopping center close to Seattle, in 1950. The tree, when erected, weighed 25 tons and required piling and cables to hold it erect. More than three thousand lights were used together with other decorations, which were placed with the aid of a helicopter. Minneapolis has become widely known for its tree built with pipes driven into a telephone pole. Small trees are inserted in the pipes to produce a spectacular man-made tree.

In thousands of communities all over the land, each with its own special kind of observance, folk gather each year to light the tree that is as sturdy as faith, as high as hope, and as wide as love, with the sign of the cross on every branch. This is the song that Christmas sings in the heart of America.

The National Community Christmas Tree, Washington, D. C. (U.S. Forest Service)

CHAPTER XII

Baubles and Tinsel

BAUBLES AND TINSEL are the stuff of which magic is made, for there is something truly magical about a Christmas tree. No tree in nature, the world over, can compare with this wondrous evergreen, decked with all the sparkle and splendor of man's imagination. Add to it the inspiration of light and the result is something quite defiant of description in ordinary words.

In 1848, when the Christmas tree was still a novelty in England, the editor of the *Illustrated London News* offered his readers an enchanting story about Dr. Claudius Shillingkite's marvelous tree in the old city of Cologne, written by R. H. Horne. To read it is to wish that the golden age of childhood might be less fleeting in our short existence. The description of the ornaments will ever serve to stir our imagination as we seek to do something original when we trim our own trees.

An old wine barrel covered with glazed paper and gold leaf was transformed into an enormous vase which "seemed to be made all of ivory." An immense fir tree was set in this container "which rose up into a succession of expansive branches, putting out their arms in varied lengths, so as to form the outline of a fine pyramid." Flame like the sparkling of steel or glass, light from numerous candles, and "lamps of scarlet and violet and green, sometimes like little, brilliant peeping stars" glowed all over the tree. "Minute fairies dressed in white . . . floated about in the air all round the tree, so as almost to touch it. Little elves dressed in short jackets, made of the peel of russet apples . . . popped in and out of the openings between the boughs.

"Grapes, both white and red, hung in large bunches beside clusters of dried raisins . . . Now and then a wind seemed to shake the boughs, and down fell a shower of nuts and sugar plums of all sizes, shapes and colors, and rattled all over the floor . . . Golden oranges and silver apples, rings and bracelets of all sorts of jewelled fashions, and sugar work in all sorts of color and devices, dangled by invisible threads." Each laden bough held a new surprise. There was a tier of "small picture books and toys" which looked as if they had grown out of the needles.

As if this were not enough for childish eyes, there were "stages made of straw resting on the heavier boughs" featuring "a field in harvest time,

complete with peasants and carts carrying away corn," all in miniature. "Four lions and four lambs in a green meadow" danced a quadrille with music made by "goldfinches and nightingales . . . perched on the backs of slumbering hawks and purring cats." It seemed as if the whole world were unfolding as "a wonderful manufactory, full of machines and wheels at work" came into view. A soldier complete with his helmet held a muzzle and chain as he danced with a pole in his hands, "while a brown bear sat near him, holding the end of the chain with one hand and a Christmas pie in the other." And the setting on each bough seemed even more wonderful and perfect in every detail as the children looked on in utter amazement. A ship moved over the waves of the sea and passed out of sight. St. George and the dragon were there too, along with a forest scene showing a Bengal tiger playing chess with a young man. There were little men building a temple and two hostile armies on another plateau arrayed for battle. This was a disturbing element amid this wonderful world of peace. As it turned out, the battle ended when a workman dropped a stone between the two warring chieftains.

Dr. Shillingkite was overjoyed as he watched the reactions of this own children and those whom he had invited to see the tree. Philosopher that he was, he summed it all up as he pointed to another scene "where Turks of baked dough and currants, and Jews who rejoice in preserved citron faces . . . dressed in light yellow robes of fresh lemon peel, sit under the same tent with Christians . . . around an egg, painted like the terrestrial globe." The ideal world was here in miniature and all the lessons to be learned were sugar-coated to appeal to the fancy of the children, but each was rich in meaning.

Those who would pursue old traditions and customs in the selection of Christmas tree ornaments will find inspiration in the gifts which the shepherds of the medieval miracle and mystery plays brought to the Christ Child. These included bells, a gourd flask, a spoon with which to eat pottage, a pipe, a type of flute or horn, a nuthook, a cape, a hood, a bob of cherries, a ball. One of the shepherds, obviously a comic character, had only a pair of his wife's stockings to offer the Child. Could this be the inspiration for hanging stockings by the chimney so that the Christ Child might fill them with gifts?

In Provence, little clay figures of peasants and tradesmen known as *santons* are used in the Christmas Cribs. All the villagers bring some useful gift, representative of their trade or craft, to the Christ Child. Eggs were always among the offerings to any newborn child, with the wish that he or she should be whole as an egg. In later generations Christmas trees were decorated with eggshells elaborately painted and ornamented. This custom was carried out both at Christmas and Easter and is still a fascinating hobby with those who delight in the unusual and enjoy perpetuating old folk customs.

Angels had a place on the tree along with the star of Bethlehem. In the early days, these and all the other decorations used were handmade, including

Home-made ornaments gave simple charm to Christmas trees in the Victorian Era. Arranged by Mrs. Ray Knowlton

Espaliered trees made of red cedar inspired by *A Partridge in a Pear Tree*. Made by Mrs. L. P. Keeler

The festive tree in all its splendor. Arranged by Mrs. Neil M. MacLaren

Sweet gum fruits were used for color on this tree made of branches of concolor fir set in a metal container by Mrs. Douglas Chandler

Ornaments made of styrofoam ornamented with sequins, beads, glitter, and "what have you" provided fun for the family of Mrs. Charles L. Johnson

Espaliered tree of evergreen roping tacked on garage door in two units so door can be opened easily. Arranged by Mrs. Robert Moore

A variety of fruits and ornaments cut from metal foil give a colorful and festive flair to this tubbed evergreen for outdoor use. Arranged by Mrs. Henry H. Hazen, Jr.

the candles. Every scrap of copper, silver, leather, cloth, paper, straw, cotton, and other materials was utilized to create fanciful ornaments.

As the popularity of the tree spread into England and America, a new industry was developed in the Thuringian Mountains of Germany where the peasants made a wide variety of blown glass ornaments by hand. In addition to balls and ovals, there were many unusual forms and shapes of delicately fashioned glass attesting to the skill and ingenuity of the various makers. Unfortunately, because of their fragility, few of the glass ornaments of the early nineteenth century remain.

The old way

An account of popular Christmas tree ornaments appearing in *Harper's Bazaar* in 1869 included the "snow-clad veteran, Santa Claus, his bag emptied of its treasures with which he has adorned the tree: globes, fruits, and flowers of colored glass, bright tin reflectors, and innumerable grotesque figures suspended by a rubber string." There were "clowns with cap and bells, funny little men concealing their faces behind funnier masks, as they spring up and down; Bismarck leaping upon Napoleon's shoulders, exaggerated seraphim with flapping wings, and strange-looking old women with heads larger than their bodies." Historical figures of prime importance mingled freely with those of the story books.

In the little glass-making town of Lauscha, in Central Germany, a century ago, the making of ornaments was a cottage industry. As the demand increased the industry spread to other glass-making towns of Central Germany until it became the sole occupation of these peasants. Often they worked under most primitive conditions and were poorly paid. Using glass tubing and a Bunsen burner, the father and older sons blew the round bubbles. Other members of the family coated the interior with a silvering solution, so that the color applied to the outer surface would reflect light. The ornaments were dried overnight on nails fastened to boards which hung from the ceiling. Then they were dipped in lacquer of every available color and decorated with fancy designs. The final step was to cut the long stem on each ornament and insert a metal cap so that they could be hung with ease.

The first ornaments were brought to America by families emigrating from Germany and England, who included them in the prized possessions they brought with them. Later they were imported for sale.

Germany had no competition in the production of Christmas ornaments until 1925. Then the Japanese began to produce them in large quantities for export to this country. Later, Czechoslovakia entered the field, sending many fancy kinds of ornaments to America. By the middle 1930's more than 250 million handmade Christmas tree ornaments were being imported annually.

The Corning Glass Works entered the tree ornament business in 1939 when the outbreak of World War II cut off the supply from abroad. By utilizing

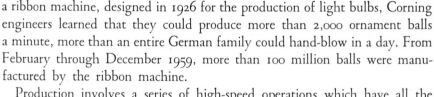

a ribbon machine, designed in 1926 for the production of light bulbs, Corning engineers learned that they could produce more than 2,000 ornament balls a minute, more than an entire German family could hand-blow in a day. From February through December 1959, more than 100 million balls were manufactured by the ribbon machine.

Production involves a series of high-speed operations which have all the magic of the decorated tree. A thin, continuous ribbon of hot glass flows over molds at great speed. Simultaneously, as each mold is positioned, a puff of compressed air on the molten ribbon shapes the ornament uniformly within the mold. Shaping is only the first of many steps in the creation of a finished ornament. As they come off the machine they are clear glass, ranging in diameter from 1¾ to 5 inches. Tests are made on sample bulbs to insure proper wall thickness and general uniformity. Then the crystal clear ornaments are silvered on the inside with a solution of silver nitrate to provide a mirror background for the lacquer applied later to the outside. Naturally, red is the most popular lacquer color, with blue ranking second. After the balls are trimmed, metal catches are attached for hanging the ornaments.

The finished balls then are shipped to decorators where stars, frosting, stripes and other designs are applied by machine or by hand. Then the finished ornaments are ready for store counters all over America. The shapes of ornaments manufactured on the ribbon machine are not as limited as might be supposed in this high-speed operation. By using a variety of molds, bell, oval, ball, top, teardrop, tree shapes, spear points, and various other kinds are produced. In spite of their fragile appearance, these mass-produced tree ornaments are much tougher than those made by hand. Because of their uniform thickness, they can be shipped without fear of breakage.

A personal touch is added to these glass balls when they are hand-decorated at home, using the names of members of the family or designs of various kinds. Thus, the age-old pleasure of having some home-made ornaments is not entirely lost, since these solid-color glass ornaments can be embellished with ease to create charming and original effects.

Flowers made of paper or cloth have been favorite forms of decoration for the Christmas tree for several centuries. Of all flowers, the rose for its superb form and color, its associations with the Virgin and the legend of the Christmas rose, continues to be a prime favorite. The tradition recorded that all the trees burst into bloom on the night that Christ was born adds further significance to the rose as a decoration. It was a favorite flower 2,000 years ago. The ease with which paper roses can be made and the warm pink and red tones of this cherished flower further add to its appeal. Conventionalized flowers of infinite variety and form, made according to the skill and ingenuity of the individual designer, are also a part of the decorations in many European countries.

The new way

Testing balls for size and quality insures the durability of machine-made ornaments

Attractive and durable packaging makes shipping and handling ornaments easy

White or colored paint is easy to apply to make personalized ornaments for your own tree

Finished ornaments are checked by a Corning technician. (Photo Corning Glass Works)

Cone tree in rich tones of brown made on frames of hardware wire. Various kinds of pine, fir, larch and hemlock cones, pods from arborvitae, beech and rhododendron combined with acorns. Made by Mrs. Edward Woll

A Christmas tree trimmed with fresh flowers, especially carnations or an arrangement of these fragrant blossoms combined with candles to simulate a tree, is an innovation of recent years. To make a carnation tree, small glass tubes with rubber caps (such as are used by florists for orchids) are filled with water and fastened to the branches with wire. As flowers fade, they can be easily replaced. In making such a tree, be sure not to place apples near the carnations, as these fruits exude a gas which shortens the life of the flowers. Fresh flowers usually last several days, depending on their condition when purchased and the temperature of the room. If the stems are steeped in water overnight and kept in a cool room, they will be well conditioned for this type of use. Red, white, and variegated varieties create a striking effect when used together.

Clear

A miniature tree using the blooms arranged with their own foliage or gilded material is also effective. Combined with candles, such as the vigil light type, delightful table trees can be made. Fresh flowers or dried materials, including fruits, offer unusual possibilities from both the symbolic and decorative points of view. Fresh or artificial flowers used on topiary trees are also pleasing to the eye.

Cones of all types are not only appropriate but highly decorative because of their intricate form, pleasing texture, long-lasting qualities, and their association with the various types of evergreens. Many legends are associated with cones. In Sicily, it is believed that the form of a hand is to be seen when a pine cone is split lengthwise. It symbolizes the hand of Jesus blessing the pine which had saved Him during the flight into Egypt by screening Him and His mother from Herod's soldiers.

Untrimmed

Cones are receptacles for the seed of evergreens and aid in its dispersal. Sometimes it is possible to obtain the top of a mature tree with the cones attached to use at Christmas, and nothing could be more beautiful. The hemlock and the larch produce tiny cones, while those of the white pine are elongated, ranging from 5 inches to nearly a foot. Cones of the redwood and pinon pine are rounded and most appealing in coloring and form. Whether used in their natural color or sprayed silver or gold, or used with other materials to make elaborate ornaments, they are always striking in their effect.

With hook on

The apple may be said to be among the oldest symbolic decorations used on an evergreen tree. From the apples came our baubles of the present day. Dried apples strung with a needle and kitchen string make attractive chains of *schnits,* as they were called in Pennsylvania. Apples were quartered, dried, and sprinkled with sulphur to keep the color light. A newspaper account from Tiffin, Ohio, January 1, 1857, described a tree with "vergoldeten sepfeln," gilded apples. Fresh apples are not as easy to attach to a tree as are the various artificial types commonly sold today. These can be kept from year to year and, when combined with other artificial fruits, are highly decorative.

Lacquered
and decorated

We read of trees decorated with eggs brightly painted and ornamented dating back a century or more. Dr. M. L. Herr of Lancaster, Pennsylvania, delighted his friends and neighbors by making a four-horse team complete with harness and reins, out of eggs. By their very pleasing shape and their fragile appearance eggs were a challenge to the ingenuity of intrepid decorators. Empty eggshells with decalcomania pictures pasted on the sides require patience and deftness, but even more challenging is the task of creating three-dimensional ornaments. Dr. Wilbur J. Kingwill of Newton, Massachusetts, an Episcopal rector, has developed his Christmas egg ornament hobby into a little business and has shipped these shimmering decorations safely all the way to Japan.

In the Dutch country of Pennsylvania where many old traditions have been cherished and kept alive, "Matzabaum, moshey and bellyguts" were favorite confections for Christmas a century and a half ago. Matzabaum is "a wonderful good" cookie or cake, while the other two items belong definitely to the realm of candy, but all are tasty. The name matzabaum is derived from the German *marzipan* or marchpane, a candy made of pounded almonds. In the Dutch country the "pan" was dropped and "baum," or tree, added, because this fancy bit was widely used to decorate the Christmas tree.

These cookies were cut from clay, wooden, or tin molds made in the shape of butterflies, birds, fish, animals, and "such-like." Dried or baked at home and made of sugar, eggs, spices, and finely chopped nuts, they were among the most delicious of cookies. Those made of starch and elaborately decorated were primarily for the tree. Simon Snyder Rathvon, writing in the Lancaster *Weekly Intelligencer* December 28, 1881, was recording his memoirs of earlier days when he wrote: "They were made of white dough, and at last two kinds: one containing sweetening and the other none . . . They were embellished with animals, trees, birds, flowers, bushes, men, women and children, pressed in a sort of 'bold relief' upon the one side, and they were gaudily painted with red, yellow, green, blue, etc., and when the youngsters commenced sucking them, for the small quantity of sugar they contained, their hands and their faces from their mouths to their eyes presented a ludicrous aspect of commingled daubery."

Gingerbread cookies in all kinds of shapes, particularly gingerbread men, were popular tree decorations made at home in bygone days. Brightened with sugar designs, they were all the more tasty and doubtless there were few left when the tree was taken down. Louise LaGorce tells in her delightful book, *The Christmas Cookie Tree,* how she set up her favorite kind of tree at the Corcoran Art Gallery in Washington, D. C., several years ago. The following year, she decorated a 15-foot tree for the lobby of the Mayflower Hotel, using two hundred cookies. The children wanted to eat them, the

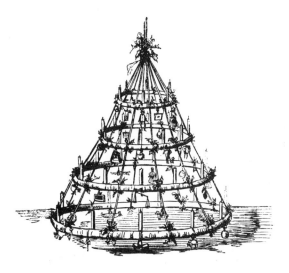

Crinoline Christmas tree made from hoopskirt frame, 1856

Espaliered tree made on a wire frame using hemlock greens and cones with artichokes for accent. Mrs. Charles L. Johnson.

Arborvitae seed pods and wild everlastings used to make a topiary tree. Mrs. Gordon W. Roaf

Tubbed yew trees, wreaths and roping of boxwood at entrance to the Howland residence

Pewter containers filled with fruits, berries, and sprigs of pine make an early American pyramid. Mrs. Hollis Gray

Plastic flower containers form the foundation of this "made" tree of boxwood, holly, pine, nuts, and fruits. Arranged by Dick Van Dusen

Starfish and various kinds of sea shells make the most natural of ornaments for this room-size tree. Arranged by Mrs. Richard Johnson

women inquired how to make them, and the men stood back and enjoyed them. The cookie tree stole everybody's heart.

Like popcorn, the flavorsome cranberry did double duty at Christmas time in the Victorian era when the berries were widely used on strings for decoration. Sometimes they were combined with popcorn to make strings of striking contrast.

Sweets, sugarplums, candy canes, marzipan, ribbon candy, peppermint lozenges, and a dozen other kinds make the kind of tree that children really love. All kinds of hard candy wrapped individually in fancy paper or packed in tiny baskets, as well as paper "horns of plenty" and tarletan bags belong on the tree too.

Doughnuts may appear to be strange ornaments for a tree, but "krentzlens" or "grenslins," as they were known to the Pennsylvania Germans, were an essential part of a nineteenth-century tree in many a farmhouse. They were called Christmas cake and made in several shapes.

For generations, dolls of every description and kind, in miniature, have had their place in the list of ornaments. Those cut out of paper, others of papier-mâché, cloth, sometimes stuffed or made of clay, glass, wood, or even corn husks depending on the era in which they were made, rate high among heirlooms with which to trim the tree.

Popcorn, easy to make and string with a needle and white string, adds a nostalgic touch. Before fancier garlands became so easy to obtain, it was used by the yard and sometimes colored. Balls made with molasses for glue were old-time favorites, but they were usually "snitched" before the tree was taken down.

Fruits, fresh or dried, sometimes ornamented, as well as artificial forms in glass, plastic, sugar paste, and other materials including plums, apples, oranges, lemons, figs, grapes, raisins, strawberries, cherries have a sound heritage. Nuts of every available kind, or just the shells, gaily painted or wrapped in gold or silver foil, or colored paper, or brightly painted, are among the oldest of ornaments for the tree.

Decorations inspired by national customs give us an even closer look into the traditions of Christmas. In the Ukraine, a favorite ornament is a spider perched on his web and his presence is as desirable as it is significant. In the great treasure house of folklore, there is a story about a poor woman who obtained a tree for her children but had no ornaments for it. Her grief was turned to joy when she awoke on Christmas morning to find that a spider had spun his webs all over the tree; the light falling on them turned the webs to silver, hence the origin of tinsel. You can make a spider from beads of various sizes and a web from pipe cleaners.

Tinsel means almost any kind of decoration that glitters, but we usually think of it as strings or garlands of metallic material. Today, we have it in

nontarnishable forms. Icicles, snow, and "glitter" in a variety of forms add their own brilliance whether the source be diamond dust, special kinds of sand, bits of glass, mica, or other materials. Cotton batting to simulate snow gives a touch of realism, but it is a fire hazard.

The inspiration of using straw comes straight from the manger and its decorative possibilities are truly amazing. Animals, birds, dolls, mobiles, garlands, angels are but a few of the possibilities. Many fanciful and charming ornaments made from straw have come to us from the Scandinavian countries.

Toys, the old and the quaint, sometimes crudely fashioned or elaborately molded and perfect in every detail, reflect the progress of mankind in every era. To attempt to list them is like carrying coals to Newcastle.

Bells and Christmas are synonymous, for they are the makers of the joyous sounds that have announced the glad tidings in every village for hundreds of years. Tolling the bell for an hour before midnight on Christmas Eve was known as tolling the devil's knell, for it was claimed that he died when Christ was born. Made of gingerbread, candy, metal, wood, glass, or paper, they belong on the trees whether it is set up indoors or out. The folding paper bells of red or green tissue became a new fashion in decorating just before the turn of the century.

Figurines, notably those of the Bambino, Mary, and Joseph, and all that wonderful assemblage that belongs to the Christmas Crib including the wise men, make our heads literally swim at the very thought of unpacking them all for next Christmas. Those who collect angels or miniature animals or any other kind of figurines often find a way of placing some of their treasures on the tree.

Birds, real or imaginary, made of dough or cloth, straw, paper, or metal, make charming and unusual decorations, and a tree on which they are featured can be as unusual as it is colorful.

Oyster shells, snail shells, and other kinds of sea shells found along the shore have possibilities known best to those who have used them. A visitor to the south of France wrote of a tree in which shells were filled with oil and tiny wicks were floated in them to produce a flickering light.

Bows and tassels, chains and garlands, and dazzlingly different kinds of stars and snowflakes belong in the category of the commonplace or the unusual, depending on how they are made.

This do-it-yourself age in which we live has opened many an avenue to those who like to make things of an ornamental or decorative nature. Why make ornaments when so many hundreds of kinds are manufactured both here and abroad? "You can often buy them cheaper than you can make them, especially if you figure the time involved." Yet half the joy of any family celebration comes from the participation of the family itself, and this fact is the very essence of the prime "feast of the heart and the home."

There is no limit to the materials that can be used. Paper drinking cups can be the basis for a doll, an angel, a windmill, a miniature tree, or what have you. Yarn for dolls, garlands, and streamers, pipe cleaners for all sorts of figures human and imaginary; wooden spools and beads, metal foil and bits of cloth—there is no end to the stuff of which ornaments can be made. Waste materials like wood shavings, ice cream and lollipop sticks, odd-sized boxes, cartons of every description, dividers from egg crates, wrappings, bits of ribbon, stoppers, bottle caps, even bits of colored glass—everything has a use. Paper and a pair of scissors can be the answer to all your needs, for marvelous indeed are the creations that can arise. See what the button box has to offer. A look along the wayside in the woods or at the beach will produce pods, straw, seashells, pebbles, feathers, and such unlikely things as corn husks, driftwood, and twigs.

Collectors of various objects sometimes display them on their trees at Christmas, creating unusual effects. Silver spoons tied with ribbon decorated a tree in an antique shop. Another decorated with hair ribbons of various colors, one featuring garlands of tulle in a dress designer's shop, safety pins in clusters and chains, a collection of china and pottery poodles, and a tree of unmatched earrings are but a few of the farfetched ways of prettying up an evergreen.

During the past century the Christmas tree has blossomed out in such varied array that we might wonder if there is anything new that can be added to its already overburdened branches. Some believe the decorations on a tree should be tied in with the setting of the individual house. For others, there is a fascination in trimming the tree in the spirit and tradition of one's ancestral country. Then there are those who are ever seeking the unusual. But new-fashioned or old-fashioned, overdone or trimly tailored, a foot high or reaching to the ceiling, it matters not; everyone decorates his own Christmas tree to suit his fancy. That's what makes the Christmas tree such fun. There are dozens of practical how-to-do-it manuals on the magazine stands each year at Christmas to inspire those who want the latest wrinkles.

See the List of Children's Books About the Christmas Tree at the back of this book for additional inspiration for ideas and techniques.

Espalier tree—wire frame using leucothoe leaves, sumac fruits for terminal points, and artichokes for accent. Arranged by Mrs. Charles Johnson

Table tree trimmed with artificial fruits and foliage, lights and gold punchinello ribbon. Arranged by Mrs. George E. Taylor

Candles and cookies on a spruce top tailored with cut branches for symmetry set on gilded cardboard by Mrs. Harold Breeding

Cone-shaped frame of chicken wire filled with loose spruce branches. Ornaments of pink Christmas wrapping paper. Arranged by Mrs. Llewellyn I. Thomas

CHAPTER XIII

More Ideas for Your Christmas Tree

TRADITION is deeply rooted and far-reaching with most of us. Thus, a Christmas tree has come to mean an evergreen of some type, decorated according to the taste and fancy of the individual who plans it. Even after a hundred years of popularity, the conventional Christmas tree still holds top place in our hearts. However, during the past two decades decorators, flower arrangers, and ingenious housewives have been dreaming up new and unusual kinds of trees. Using every conceivable kind of material, both live and artificial, they have contrived trees such as Solomon never dreamed of and nature could hardly produce.

In the days following the Civil War, individuals like Grandmamma Shuptrine of Mississippi were early innovators. The dear old mammy used the myrtle bush in the yard as the place to hang her grandchildren's Christmas gifts, to keep them from cluttering up her small cabin. Hers was a "paper bag" tree, since the presents were placed in bags. The children made a scramble for them and soon learned that the size of the bag was no indication of the worth of its contents. Medical students in Philadelphia dreamed up the novelty of an anatomic tree to amuse their professor. An overenthusiastic boy in the 1850's suggested the hoop skirt frame from his sister's closet as a pattern for a tree. But these were exceptional ideas even then.

It used to be traditional at Christmas to use an evergreen, set on the floor or on a table. In Germany the custom of large boughs placed against the wall, or suspended from the ceiling, was an early fashion. This gave way to the use of live trees of various sizes in pots, a custom that became popular in many European cities. Often these trees were grown on from year to year in their containers.

In creating new and original ways to make and use Christmas trees to fit the needs of present-day living, many fresh ideas for decoration have evolved. These "made" trees can be used where space is limited, and they can be adapted to locations where the conventional tree in the round would not be suitable or desirable. Ingenuity, imagination, and the desire to create are the

basic requirements for making a new and different kind of Christmas tree. For those not inclined to dream up something new, there are dozens of tested ideas that can be adapted. With only a few yards of tinsel and a handful of baubles you can outline a tree on a window or a wall. Paper and scissors will produce any number of designs, either flat or in the round. A cone of hardware wire plus some evergreens, nuts, or seed pods will result in a smartly tailored effect.

Today, we have topiary trees, espaliered forms, some that look like mobiles, and trees made of cones, nuts, seed pods or dried flowers. Picturesquely curved bare twigs or branches from trees lend themselves to many kinds of decorative treatment. Where a large picture window is available two trees are sometimes used. One is placed inside and the other outside to give the illusion of a single tree. Then there are trees cut from paper or cloth or fashioned on wire frames to create the effect of a silhouette.

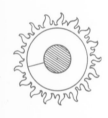

Trees for various rooms in the house can be adapted to the décor of the individual room. While earlier generations have largely stressed the use of ornament and decoration, the present trend is concerned with the infinite variety of forms of the tree which are possible.

Turning to the liturgical symbolism of the Christmas season, we find inspiration for Christmas trees that help prepare the way for the great day. The Advent tree and the Jesse tree can be considered as two distinct types, or they can be combined in a variety of ways to provide children and grown-ups with a fresh approach to the meaning of Christmas.

In many European countries the season of Advent (the four weeks preceding Christmas) is looked upon as the period of preparation for the birth of the Christ Child. An old custom widely practiced in parts of Germany and the Scandinavian countries is woven around the lighting of a candle on each of the four Sundays preceding Christmas. Sometimes the candles are placed in a wreath of evergreens or on a small tree. Symbols cut from paper and other materials are colored or onamented. Each day an emblem associated with a particular feast or liturgical observance is placed on the wreath or tree. Simple stands designed in the form of trees serve to hold the candles. This idea is sometimes combined with another symbolic tree known as the Jesse tree.

A comparatively new idea for decorating Christmas trees is to use various Old Testament symbols cut out of cardboard, fancy paper, metal foil, or any other suitable material to make a Jesse tree. This concept of a Christmas tree provides a fresh approach to the Old Testament stories and the events leading up to the birth of the Christ Child. The prophet Isaiah had foretold that the Saviour would be born from the root of Jesse; he would spring from the root of this symbolic tree and would sit on the Throne of David. In the birth of Christ that prophecy was fulfilled. With the revival of interest in liturgical

Advent tree, gilded wood frame. Purple ribbon used with candles and wheat clusters. Adapted from a design by Zelda Wyatt Schulke and arranged by Mrs. Gordon W. Roaf

Oranges, gilded ivy leaves, and small cones combined to create a pyramid. A similar concept was used by the Moravians in Pennsylvania two centuries ago. Mrs. R. C. Dixon

Oak leaves in warm brown tones adapted to a door tree create a most unusual effect.

Animal cracker tree to delight children made on a paper cone with gold paper cutouts for additional decoration. Mrs. Gordon W. Roaf

Red and white carnations combined with vigil lights lend color and fragrance to a Christmas table. Arranged by Mrs. Louis Phaneuf

Fresh ivy leaves with butterflies remind us of the golden legends which told of birds and insects that hovered about the night Christ was born. Mrs. Eric Meakin

Kissing ball suspended in a bird cage stand with colored glass balls for a baroque touch. Mrs. Elwood W. Schafer

Topiary tree made of yew branches trimmed with ribbons, cloth flowers, and glass baubles. Mrs. Elwood W. Schafer

symbolism, the Jesse tree is growing in popularity among families throughout the country. Cardboard cut-outs of many of these symbols are available from the Liturgical Press, Collegeville, Minnesota.

A simple cut-out representing the sun depicts Christ as the sun of justice, banishing darkness, and bringing life and light. The Law of Moses is represented in the tablets which God gave to Moses on Mount Sinai. From the Royal House of David, we have the key and the six-pointed star. A silhouette of Bethlehem, which means "House of Bread," the root of Jesse, Jonah and the whale, Jacob's ladder, the Temple, the crown and scepter, the sword of Judith, and the burning bush are among the cut-outs included on this novel type of tree. Additional emblems which can be hung include Noah's ark, the Ark of the Covenant, the Altar of Holocaust, the apple, the Paschal lamb, the Pillar of Fire, and Manna. To these decorations may be added figures of Adam and Eve and other Bible characters.

Many plants, some of them tree-like in habit of growth, are utilized on Christmas trees. One of these is the so-called Jerusalem cherry. This is not a true cherry. A tropical plant related to the potato and the pepper, it has a pleasing tree-like habit. Its white flowers are followed by bright orange cherry-like fruits a little more than a half-inch in diameter. Introduced to this country more than a century ago, it has become exceedingly popular, particularly because it bears these fruits at Christmas. The name "Jerusalem cherry" may have originated from the old story of the Cherry Tree Carol. However, the fact that it has no relation to the true cherry has little significance, since the showy fruits are highly decorative and fit into the symbolism of the season.

The Norfolk Island pine, which is not a true pine but resembles one in its habit of growth and pyramidal form, bears needle-like foliage of great ornamental value. This tropical introduction makes a shapely specimen and can be readily adapted as a living Christmas tree.

Another plant of special significance at Christmas which can be used for a tree is the fragrant rosemary. This plant, native to the Mediterranean and widely grown in Europe, has been associated with the Virgin Mary down through the ages. Its pungent foliage and needle-like leaves are particularly appealing, and it was a cherished item in many an Elizabethan nosegay. The old legend has it that the flowers were originally white and turned blue when Our Lady washed her cloak and spread it on the rosemary bush to dry.

With normal care, a freshly cut balsam or Douglas fir, a cedar, a pine, and many other types of evergreens offered in markets can be expected to hold their needles for the Christmas holidays. However, the long distance between sources of supply, distribution points, and markets constitutes a problem in keeping cut trees in prime condition. Of necessity, trees are often cut several months before Christmas and placed in cold storage. During shipment they are protected, but once they reach the market, they often get rough treatment. Thus, it is important to select your tree with care and keep it cool and moist until you are ready to use it indoors.

Evergreens begin to lose moisture as soon as they are cut. As trees become dry, needles fall and their rich green color fades. When you purchase your tree, store it in a cool, protected place away from sun and wind. Rain or snow will keep it fresh, or you can stand it in a bucket of water and sprinkle the branches daily. A fresh cut made with a saw on the butt before placing it in water will aid greatly in the absorption of moisture.

When you are ready to set up your tree indoors, give some thought to its location, not only from the point of view of appearance, but also its position with relation to radiators, television, fireplaces, and other sources of heat. Even though a fresh cut is made in the butt end and the tree is placed in water, it will still tend to dry out as moisture is given off through the needles. Water at the base of the stem must be constant. Most Christmas tree holders do not have adequate water capacity. Actually a large pail, vase, jardiniere, or other waterproof container is preferable.

Check for all possible fire hazards. When used, candles should be for ornament only, and never lighted. Electric wiring and sockets must be in perfect condition, since worn or frayed wiring can be a serious hazard. Also, badly made or loose connections are a menace. Metal foil in the form of icicles and other trimmings must be kept away from light sockets. Flimsy ornaments should never be placed too near lights. Cotton batting to conceal wiring is also undesirable. In short, every possible precaution should be taken to avoid and to eliminate fire hazards.

When live trees are used indoors, they require constant watering and should be removed to the open as soon after the holidays as possible. Sometimes they can be stored in a cool place to await planting, or they can be kept in their containers until spring; but they must not be allowed to dry out.

After the holidays when trees are discarded, some communities make an occasion of burning the greens on Twelfth Night. This ceremony had its origin in several ancient practices of lighting fires at Epiphany. In Normandy the day was the occasion for a bonfire to mark the end of Christmas. In parts of rural England it was the custom for the farmer and his servants to meet in a field newly sown with wheat where thirteen fires were lit, one of which was larger than all the rest. Around the big fire, they gathered and drank a glass of cider to the success of the harvest. In Herefordshire the burning of the bush was a ritual on Epiphany Eve. The "bush" was a globe made of hawthorn, hung with mistletoe, and kept in the farm kitchen throughout the year. After it was burned, a new bush was made and the ends of its branches were seared with the fire of the old one.

Sculptured espalier trees made with cones and pods. Arranged by Mrs. Chester Cook. Courtesy, Museum of Fine Arts, Boston

Actually, it has long been customary to allow the Christmas wreaths and garlands to remain in place until Candlemas Day, when they are taken down and burned. Or, as the poet Herrick has expressed it:

Down with the Rosemary and Bayes,   The Holly hitherto did sway;
Down with the Mistleto;   Let Box now domineere
Instead of Holly, now up-raise   Until the dancing Easter Day,
The greener Box for show.   Or Easter's Eve appeare.

Burning Christmas trees is often the most practical way of disposing of them, but there are many ways in which they can be used in the home garden. A discarded evergreen makes an ideal feeding station for birds. Various kinds of seed, suet, bread, fruit, and other foods can be tied to the branches to provide needed bird food. Entire trees make good windbreaks to protect plants from both wind and sun, or the branches can be removed to provide protective cover for low evergreen shrubs and perennials.

CHAPTER XIV

Stories and Legends of the Tree

THE FIR TREE

Hans Christian Andersen

OUT in the woods stood a nice little Fir tree. The place he had was a very good one; the sun shone on him; as to fresh air, there was enough of that, and round him grew many large-sized comrades, pines as well as firs. But the little Fir wanted so very much to be a grown-up tree.

He did not think of the warm sun and of the fresh air; he did not care for the little cottage children that ran about and prattled when they were in the woods looking for wild strawberries. The children often sat down near the young tree and said, "Oh, how pretty he is! What a nice little fir!" But this was what the Tree could not bear to hear.

At the end of a year he had shot up a good deal, and after another year he was another long bit taller; for with fir trees one can always tell by the shoots how many years old they are.

"Oh, were I but such a high tree as the others are!" sighed he. "Then I should be able to spread out my branches, and with the tops to look into the wide world! Then would the birds build nests among my branches; and when there was a breeze, I could bend with as much stateliness as the others!"

Neither the sunbeams, nor the birds, nor the red clouds, which morning and evening sailed above them, gave the little Tree any pleasure.

In winter, when the snow lay glittering on the ground, a hare would often come leaping along, and jump right over the little Tree. Oh, that made him so angry! But two winters were past, and in the third the Tree was so large that the hare was obliged to go around it. "To grow and grow, to get older and be tall," thought the Tree—"that, after all, is the most delightful thing in the world!"

In autumn the woodcutters always came and felled some of the largest trees. This happened every year; and the young Fir tree, that had now grown to a very comely size, trembled at the sight; for the magnificent great trees fell to the earth with noise and crackling, the branches were lopped off, and the trees looked long bare; they were hardly to be recognized; and then they were laid in carts, and the horses dragged them out of the woods.

Where did they go to? What became of them?

In Spring, when the Swallows and the Storks came, the Tree asked them, "Don't you know where they have been taken? Have you not met them anywhere?"

The Swallows did not know anything about it; but the Stork looked musing, nodded his head, and said: "Yes, I think I know; I met many ships as I was flying hither from Egypt; on the ships were magnificent masts, and I venture to assert that it was they that smelt so of fir. I may congratulate you, for they lifted themselves on high most majestically!"

"Oh, were I but old enough to fly across the sea!"

When Christmas came, quite young trees were cut down, trees which often were not even as large or of the same age as this Fir tree, who could never rest, but always wanted to be off. These young trees, and they were always the finest looking, retained their branches; they were laid on carts, and the horses drew them out of the woods.

"Where are they going to?" asked the Fir.

"We know! we know!" chirped the Sparrows. "We have peeped in at the windows in the town below! The greatest splendor and the greatest magnificence one can imagine await them. We peeped through the windows, and saw them planted in the middle of the warm room, and ornamented with the most splendid things—with gilded apples, with gingerbread, with toys, and many hundred lights!"

"Oh, were I but already on the cart!" cried the Tree. "Were I in the warm room with all the splendor and magnificence! Yes; then something better, something still grander, will surely follow, or wherefore should they thus ornament me? Something better, grander, must follow—but what?"

"Rejoice in our presence!" said the Air and the Sunlight; "rejoice in thy own fresh youth!"

But the Tree did not rejoice at all; he grew and grew, and was green both winter and summer. People that saw him said, "What a fine tree!" and toward Christmas he was one of the first that was cut down. The axe struck deep into the very pitch; the Tree fell to the earth with a sigh; he felt a pang—it was like a swoon; he could not think of happiness, for he was sorrowful at being separated from his home, from the place where he had sprung up. He knew well that he should never see his

dear old comrades, the little bushes and flowers around him, any more; perhaps not even the birds! The departure was not at all agreeable.

The Tree came to himself when he was unloaded in a courtyard with the other trees, and heard a man say, "That one is splendid! we don't want the others." Then two servants in rich livery came and carried the Fir tree into a large and splendid drawing room. And the Fir tree was stuck upright in a cask that was filled with sand; but no one could see that it was a cask, for green cloth was hung all around it, and it stood on a large gaily colored carpet. Oh, how the Tree quivered! What was to happen? The servants, as well as the young ladies, decorated it. On one branch there hung little nets cut out of paper, and each net was filled with sugar-plums; and among the other boughs gilded apples and walnuts were suspended, looking as though they had grown there, and little blue and white tapers were placed among the leaves. Dolls that looked for all the world like men—the Tree had never beheld such before—were seen among the foliage, and at the very top a large star of gold tinsel was fixed. It was really splendid —beyond description splendid.

"This evening!" said they all; "how it will shine this evening!"

"Oh," thought the Tree, "if the evening were but come! If the tapers were but lighted! And then I wonder what will happen! Perhaps the other trees from the forest will come to look at me! Perhaps the Sparrows will beat against the window-panes! I wonder if I shall take root here, and winter and summer stand covered with ornaments!"

The candles were now lighted. What brightness! What splendor! The Tree trembled so in every bough that one of the tapers set fire to the foliage. It blazed up splendidly.

"Help! Help!" cried the young ladies, and they quickly put out the fire.

Now the Tree did not even dare tremble. What a state he was in. He was so uneasy lest he should lose something of his splendor, that he was quite bewildered amidst the glare and brightness; when suddenly both folding doors opened, and a troop of children rushed in as if they would upset the Tree. The older persons followed quietly; the little ones stood quite still. But it was only for a moment; then they shouted so that the whole place re-echoed with their rejoicing; they danced around the Tree, and one present after the other was pulled off.

"What are they about?" thought the Tree. "What is to happen now?" And the lights burned down to the very branches, and as they burned down they were put out, one after the other, and then the children had permission to plunder the Tree. So they fell upon it with such violence that all its branches cracked; if it had not been fixed firmly in the cask, it would certainly have tumbled down.

"A story! a story!" cried the children, drawing a little fat man toward the Tree. He seated himself under it, and said: "Now we are in the shade, and the Tree can listen, too. But I shall tell only one story."

And the man told about Klumpy-Dumpy that tumbled down, who notwithstanding, came to the throne, and at last married the princess. "Yes! Yes! That's the way of the world!" thought the Fir tree, and believed it all, because the man who told the story was so good looking. "Well, well! who knows, perhaps I may fall downstairs, too, and get a princess as a wife!"

In the morning the servant and the housemaid came in.

"Now then, the splendor will begin again," thought the Fir. But they dragged him out of the room, and up the stairs into the loft; and here in a dark corner, where no daylight could enter, they left him. "What am I to do here? What shall I hear now, I wonder?" Time enough had he, too, for his reflections; for days and nights passed on, and nobody came up; and when at last somebody did come, it was only to put some great trunks in a corner out of the way. There stood the Tree quite hidden; it seemed as if he had been entirely forgotten.

"'Tis now winter out of doors!" thought the Tree. "The earth is hard and covered with snow; men cannot plant me now, and therefore I have been put up here under shelter till the springtime comes! How thoughtful that is! How kind man is, after all! If it only were not so dark here, and so terribly lonely! Not even a hare. And out in the woods it was so pleasant, when the snow was on the ground, and the hare leaped by, yes— even when he jumped over me; but I did not like it then. It is really terribly lonely here!"

"Squeak! squeak!" said a little Mouse at the same moment, peeping out of his hole. And then another little one came. They sniffed about the Fir tree, and rustled among the branches.

"It is dreadfully cold," said the Mouse. "But for that, it would be delightful here, old Fir, wouldn't it?"

"I am by no means old," said the Fir tree. "There's many a one considerably older than I am."

"Where do you come from," asked the Mice; "and what can you do?" They were so extremely curious. "Tell us about the most beautiful spot on the earth. Have you never been there? Were you never in the larder, where cheeses lie on the shelves, and hams hang from above; where one dances about on tallow candles; that place where one enters lean, and comes out again fat and portly?"

"I know no such place," said the Tree, "but I know the woods, where the sun shines, and where the little birds sing." And then he told them all about his youth; and the little Mice had never heard the like before; and they listened and said:

"Well, to be sure! How much you have seen! How happy you must have been!"

"I?" said the Fir tree, thinking over what he had himself related. "Yes, in reality those were happy times." And then he told about Christmas Eve, when he was decked out with cakes and candles.

"Oh," said the little Mice, "how fortunate you have been, old Fir tree!"

"I am by no means old," said he. "I came from the woods this winter; I am in my prime, and am only rather short for my age."

"What delightful stories you know!" said the Mice; and the next night they came with four other little Mice, who were to hear what the tree recounted; and the more he related, the more plainly he remembered all himself; and it appeared as if those times had really been happy times. "But they may still come—they may still come. Klumpy-Dumpy fell downstairs and yet he got a princess." And he thought at the moment of a nice little Birch tree growing out in the woods; to the Fir, that would be a real charming princess.

"Who is Klumpy-Dumpy?" asked the Mice. So then the Fir tree told the whole fairy tale, for he could remember every single word of it; and the little Mice jumped for joy up to the very top of the Tree. Next night two more Mice came, and on Sunday two Rats, even; but they said the stories were not interesting, which vexed the little Mice; and they, too, now began to think them not so very amusing either.

"So you know only one story?" asked the Rats.

"Only that one," answered the Tree. "I heard it on my happiest evening; but I did not then know how happy I was."

"It is a very stupid story. Don't you know one about bacon and tallow candles? Can't you tell any larder stories?"

"No," said the Tree.

"Then good-bye," said the Rats; and they went home.

At last the little Mice stayed away also;

and the Tree sighed. "After all, it was very pleasant when the sleek little Mice sat around me and listened to what I told them. Now that too is over. But I will take good care to enjoy myself when I am brought out again."

But when was that to be? Why, one morning there came a quantity of people and set to work in the loft. The trunks were moved, the Tree was pulled out and thrown—rather hard, it is true—down on the floor, but a man drew him toward the stairs, where the daylight shone.

"Now a merry life will begin again," thought the Tree and spread out his branches; but alas! they were withered and yellow. It was in a corner that he lay, among weeds and nettles. The golden star of tinsel was still on the top of the Tree, and glittered in the sunshine.

In the courtyard some of the merry children were playing who had danced at Christmas round the Fir tree, and were so glad at the sight of him. One of the youngest ran and tore off the golden star.

"Only look what is still on the ugly old Christmas tree!" said he, trampling on the branches, so that they all cracked beneath his feet.

" 'Tis over—'tis past!" said the poor Tree. "Had I but rejoiced when I had reason to do so! But now 'tis past, 'tis past!"

And the gardener's boy chopped the Tree into small pieces; there was a whole heap lying there. The wood flamed up splendidly under the large brewing copper, and it sighed so deeply! Each sigh was like a shot.

The boys played about the court, and the youngest wore the gold star on his breast which the Tree had had on the happiest evening of his life. However, that was over now—the Tree was gone, the story at an end. All, all was over; every tale must end at last.

THE MIRACLE OF THE FIR TREE

Jean Variot

ONCE upon a time on a frosty Christmas Eve, in a small village, a little boy was wandering barefooted, from house to house.

"Would anyone like to buy two small fir trees? . . . You can decorate them with bright lights and paper stars . . . It's a lot of fun for the children," the boy would cry, as he knocked on a door.

At each house, the answer was always the same:

"You've come too late, child. We've already bought our Christmas tree. Come back again next year."

And each time the boy would go away with tears in his eyes. If he didn't sell the two trees there would be nothing for his family to eat. His mother and father were both sick, and his two brothers were still babies. Albert was the only one in his family able to earn money. So, in spite of the bitter cold, he roved through the street, looking for someone to buy his fir trees. He had found the trees on the edge of the woods, just as night began to fall, at the hour when hungry wolves begin their howling.

After knocking on several doors, and receiving many blunt answers, the boy found himself at the house of Eidel, the gardner.

Can you imagine trying to sell fir trees to a man whose job it is to make them grow?

Albert knocked.

"Who is knocking at this hour?" Eidel's gruff voice replied.

By now, Albert was so afraid, he didn't dare say who he was or what he wanted.

"Who is it? Who is knocking at my door when I want to be left in peace?" grumbled Eidel, his wooden shoes clattering as he came along.

When the door opened, the boy saw a beautiful tree, glistening with gaily wrapped presents and decorations whose bright glittering lit up the deserted street.

At the other end of the room, there was a blazing fire in the hearth. And sitting near it were three children looking from the hearth to the kitchen, where a juicy Christmas turkey lay on a table just waiting to be eaten.

"What do you want, little one?" Eidel asked the boy. "What are you doing with those two stunted fir trees?"

Albert didn't answer, as he thought he had just lost his last chance to earn money.

"The cold wind is blowing in," said the gardener. "Speak up, boy, or I'll have to close the door and leave you standing there."

Eidel had a rough way of speaking, but he was a good man. Looking at poor, frightened Albert standing in the snow, without any shoes, the gardener thought of his own children. They were about the same age as this boy. "If I were not here to look after them, some wintry night, my children might be roaming the streets too," he said to himself. But kindly he asked Albert, "What can I do for you?"

"I wanted to sell my fir trees for Christmas," said Albert, "but you already have such a beautiful one."

"Never mind!" Eidel answered. "All the same, I'll buy yours." And he went to get a gold coin from the drawer where he kept his savings.

"It's too good to be true," thought Albert. "The old gardener must be playing a joke on me, or maybe it's all a dream." But when each of the children gave him a slice of turkey and their mother brought out a piping hot bowl of soup, Albert knew he wasn't dreaming.

When he had finished eating, the boy thanked the kind gardener and his family. And, happy as a lark, he started home with Eidel's dog for protection against the wolves.

On Christmas morning, after all the presents had been opened, Mrs. Eidel started cleaning up her house. She picked up all the wrappings, the ribbons, the decorations, and put them away. The she threw the two fir trees of Albert's into the street.

Her three children were playing in tne street while waiting to go to church. When they saw their mother throw the fir trees out they decided to pretend they were gardeners, just like their father. So they took the trees across the road and planted them behind the church.

Soon the church bells began to ring and crowds of people started pouring into the church. Eidel and his family were among the first to arrive. Dressed in his best clothes, Eidel sat with his wife and children in the front pew. The gardener rev-

erently asked God to watch over his family. As the choir sang the glory and wonder of Our Lord's birth, it occurred to Eidel that the Infant born in a manger is the true brother of poor children. "One can never be too kind to them," the gardener thought.

Mass was over, the candles snuffed out and the last parishioners leaving, when, all at once, the crowd outside the church gasped in amazement. High above the steeple, as straight as masts of a ship, were two fir trees, towering to the sky. And all around their thick, heavy branches, doves, as white as snow, singing the Glory of God.

(*Translated from the French by Leon King*)

THE PETERKINS' CHRISTMAS TREE

Lucretia P. Hale

EARLY in autumn the Peterkins began to prepare for their Christmas tree. Everything was done in great privacy, as it was to be a surprise to the neighbors, as well as to the rest of the family. Mr. Peterkin had been up to Mr. Bromwick's wood lot, and, with his consent, selected the tree. Agamemnon went to look at it occasionally after dark, and Solomon John made frequent visits to it mornings, just after sunrise. Mr. Peterkin drove Elizabeth Eliza and her mother that way, and pointed furtively to it with his whip; but none of them ever spoke of it to each other. It was suspected that the little boys had been to see it Wednesday and Saturday afternoons. But they came home with their pockets full of chestnuts, and said nothing about it.

At length Mr. Peterkin had it cut down and brought secretly into the Larkins' barn. A week or two before Christmas a measurement was made of it with Elizabeth Eliza's yard measure. To Mr. Peterkin's great dismay it was discovered that it was too high to stand in the back parlor.

This fact was brought out at a secret council of Mr. and Mrs. Peterkin, Elizabeth Eliza, and Agamemnon.

Agamemnon suggested that it might be set up slanting; but Mrs. Peterkin was very sure it would make her dizzy, and the candles would drip.

But a brilliant idea came to Mr. Peterkin. He proposed that the ceiling of the parlor should be raised to make room for the top of the tree.

Elizabeth Eliza thought the space would need to be quite large. It must not be like a small box, or you could not see the tree.

"Yes," said Mr. Peterkin, "I should have the ceiling lifted all across the room; the effect would be finer."

Elizabeth Eliza objected to having the whole ceiling raised, because her room was over the back parlor, and she would have no floor while the alteration was going on, which would be very awkward. Besides, her room was not very high now, and, if the floor were raised, perhaps she could not walk in it upright.

Mr. Peterkin explained that he didn't propose altering the whole ceiling, but to lift up a ridge across the room at the back part where the tree was to stand. This would make a hump, to be sure, in Elizabeth Eliza's room; but it would go across the whole room.

Elizabeth Eliza said she would not mind that. It would be like the cuddy thing that comes up on the deck of a ship, that you sit against, only here you would not have seasickness. She thought she should like it, for a rarity. She might use it for a divan.

Mrs. Peterkin thought it would come in the worn place of the carpet, and might be a convenience in making the carpet over.

Agamemnon was afraid there would be trouble in keeping the matter secret, for it would be a long piece of work for a carpenter; but Mr. Peterkin proposed having the carpenter for a day or two, for a number of other jobs.

One of them was to make all the chairs in the house of the same height, for Mrs. Peterkin had nearly broken her spine by sitting down in a chair that she had supposed was her own rocking chair, and it had proved to be two inches lower. The little boys were now large enough to sit in any chair; so a medium was fixed upon to satisfy all the family, and the chairs were made uniformly of the same height.

On consulting the carpenter, however, he insisted that the tree could be cut off at the lower end to suit the height of the parlor, and demurred at so great a change as altering the ceiling. But Mr. Peterkin had set his mind upon the improvement, and Elizabeth Eliza had cut her carpet in preparation for it.

So the folding doors into the back parlor were closed, and for nearly a fortnight before Christmas there was great litter of fallen plastering, and laths, and chips, and shavings; and Elizabeth Eliza's carpet was taken up, and the furniture had to be changed, and one night she had to sleep at the Bromwick's, for there was a long hole in her floor that might be dangerous.

All this delighted the little boys. They could not understand what was going on. Perhaps they suspected a Christmas tree, but they did not know why a Christmas tree should have so many chips, and were still more astonished at the hump that appeared in Elizabeth Eliza's room. It must be a Christmas present, or else the tree in a box.

Some aunts and uncles, too, arrived a day or two before Christmas, with some small cousins. These cousins occupied the attention of the little boys, and there was a great deal of whispering and mystery, behind doors, and under the stairs, and in the corners of the entry.

Solomon John was busy, privately making some candles for the tree. He had been collecting some bayberries, as he understood they made very nice candles, so that it would not be necessary to buy any.

The elders of the family never all went into the back parlor together, and all tried not to see what was going on. Mrs. Peterkin would go in with Solomon John, or Mr. Peterkin with Elizabeth Eliza, or Elizabeth Eliza and Agamemnon and Solomon John. The little boys and the small cousins were never allowed even to look inside the room.

Elizabeth Eliza meanwhile went into town a number of times. She wanted to consult Amanda as to how much ice cream they should need, and whether they could make it at home, as they had cream and ice. She was pretty busy in her own room; the furniture had to be changed, and the carpet altered. The "hump" was higher than she expected. There was danger of bumping her own head whenever she crossed it. She had to nail some padding on the ceiling for fear of accidents.

The afternoon before Christmas, Elizabeth Eliza, Solomon John, and their father collected in the back parlor for a council. The carpenters had done their work, and the tree stood at its full height at the back of the room, the top stretching up into the space arranged for it. All the chips and shavings were cleared away, and it stood on a neat box.

But what were they to put upon the tree?

Solomon John had brought in his supply of candles; but they proved to be very "stringy" and very few of them. It was strange how many bayberries it took to make a few candles! The little boys had helped him, and he had gathered as much as a bushel of bayberries. He had put them in water, and skimmed off the wax, according to the directions; but there was so little wax!

Solomon John had given the little boys some of the bits sawed off from the legs of the chairs. He had suggested that they should cover them with gilt paper, to answer for gilt apples, without telling them what they were for.

These apples, a little blunt at the end, and the candles, were all they had for the tree!

After all her trips into town Elizabeth Eliza had forgotten to bring anything for it.

"I thought of candles and sugar plums," she said; "but I concluded if we made caramels ourselves we should not need them. But then, we have not made caramels. The fact is, that day my head was full of my carpet. I had bumped it pretty badly, too."

Mr. Peterkin wished he had taken, instead of a fir tree, an apple tree he had seen in October, full of red fruit.

"But the leaves would have fallen off by this time," said Elizabeth Eliza.

"And the apples, too," said Solomon John.

"It is odd I should have forgotten, that day I went in on purpose to get the things," said Elizabeth Eliza, musingly. "But I went from shop to shop, and didn't know exactly what to get. I saw a great many gilt things for Christmas trees; but I knew the little boys were making the gilt apples; there were plenty of candles in the shops, but I knew Solomon John was making the candles."

Mr. Peterkin thought it was quite natural.

Solomon John wondered if it were too late for them to go into town now.

Elizabeth Eliza could not go in the next morning, for there was to be a grand Christmas dinner, and Mr. Peterkin could not be spared, and Solomon John was sure he and Agamemnon would not know what to buy. Besides, they would want to try the candles tonight.

Mr. Peterkin asked if the presents everybody had been preparing would not answer. But Elizabeth Eliza knew they would be too heavy.

A gloom came over the room. There was only a flickering gleam from one of Solomon John's candles that he had lighted by way of trial.

Solomon John again proposed going into town. He lighted a match to examine the newspaper about the trains. There were plenty of trains coming out at that hour, but none going in except a very late one. That would not leave time to do anything and come back.

"We could go in, Elizabeth Eliza and I," said Solomon John, "but we should not have time to buy anything."

Agamemnon was summoned in. Mrs. Peterkin was entertaining the uncles and aunts in the front parlor. Agamemnon wished there was time to study up something about electric lights. If they could only have a calcium light! Solomon John's candle sputtered and went out.

At this moment there was a loud knocking at the front door. The little boys, and the small cousins, and the uncles and aunts, and Mrs. Peterkin, hastened to see what was the matter.

The uncles and aunts thought somebody's house must be on fire. The door was opened, and there was a man, white with flakes, for it was beginning to snow, and he was pulling in a large box.

Mrs. Peterkin supposed it contained some of Elizabeth Eliza's purchases, so she ordered it to be pushed into the back parlor, and hastily called back her guests and the little boys into the other room. The little boys and the small cousins were sure they had seen Santa Claus himself.

Mr. Peterkin lighted the gas. The box was addressed to Elizabeth Eliza. It was from the lady from Philadelphia! She had gathered a hint from Elizabeth Eliza's letters that there was to be a Christmas tree, and had filled this box with all that would be needed.

It was opened directly. There was every kind of gilt hanging-thing, from gilt pea pods to butterflies on springs. There were shining flags and lanterns, and bird cages, and nests with birds sitting on them, baskets of fruit, gilt apples and bunches of grapes, and, at the bottom of the whole, a large box of candles and a box of Philadelphia bonbons!

Elizabeth Eliza and Solomon John could scarcely keep from screaming. The little boys and the small cousins knocked on the folding doors to ask what was the matter.

Hastily Mr. Peterkin and the rest took out the things and hung them on the tree, and put on the candles.

When all was done, it looked so well that Mr. Peterkin exclaimed:

"Let us light the candles now, and send to invite all the neighbors tonight, and have the tree on Christmas Eve!"

And so it was that the Peterkins had their Christmas tree the day before, and on Christmas night could go and visit their neighbors.

YOLKA (A LITTLE FIR TREE)

Marguerita Rudolph

THIS is a story of the farthest North, the Arctic Ocean. It is a true story, and you may read about it in Russian books. What is more, you may see the proof of it in the Leningrad Arctic Museum.

In the year 1937, three well-manned Russian ships went on a Polar expedition and were forced to spend the winter in the Arctic Ocean. The ships were frozen into the ice and the men were not able to sail them back to land. Thick strong heaps of ice surrounded the ships and held them fast. The temperature dipped as low as it could be measured and everybody aboard the ships knew that it wouldn't warm up for many months, for it was only the end of December. There was complete darkness all around day and night, for in the Arctic the sun doesn't appear in the sky at all during the winter months. But the men were not downhearted. Most of them had sailed in the Arctic before and they were prepared to endure the winter. Besides, all the scientists were too busy to fear or worry, they continued to make important observations of ice and wind and atmosphere; they attended to their instruments and made

complicated calculations. After work there was time for rest and even for fun aboard; there were radio programs, books and games.

The writer in the crew, Konstantin Badigin, wrote long articles about life in the Arctic. Usually the articles were too long and the radio engineer, Nikolai Bekasov, kept complaining.

"I beg you, Badigin, not to write so much! Remember, I have to relay all you write by radio!" But Badigin kept writing.

By the end of December the men aboard one of the ships, *The Sadko,* began to talk about the holiday preparations going on in people's homes, on land.

"I imagine," said Badigin, wistfully, "that people at home must be getting Christmas trees and decorating them with bright colored lights and toys while we are aboard ship, a thousand kilometers from the nearest forest of fir trees."

"That is nothing to worry about," answered Nikolai Bekasov, the radio engineer. "Use your imagination, Badigin. Pretend there is a fresh green fir tree aboard and you won't need to write an article about it."

"Don't make fun of me," said Badigin. "What sort of a celebration could we have without a real tree?" Then neither of them said anything more.

The next day a rumor spread aboard that there would be a tree.

"A tree?" questioned Pavel, the ship's cook. "Here, in the icy ocean?" He pushed his cook's hat back and scratched his head thoughtfully. Badigin, the writer was specially curious.

"How could it have come to the Arctic?" he asked, trying to be practical. "Where could it have grown?"

"I don't know anything about it," answered Bekasov indifferently.

"But, who does know?" asked Yefremov, the captain's assistant. "And do you suppose Grandpa Frost will come around with presents for us, too! My, my, what surprises!"

"Yefremov, you greedy pig!" criticized Bekasov, and he shook his head and pointed his finger.

On the eve of the holiday, New Year's Eve, the doors of the ship's wardroom were flung wide open. The wardroom was the finest cabin on the ship and was used for eating and resting and meetings and entertainment. When the sailors came into the wardroom they noticed that the tables were set for a supper with unusual care, a savory odor of cooking was in the air, and in the middle of the room there was —unmistakably a Christmas tree!

"Yolka!" Badigin shouted in surprise, and everyone stared in astonishment at the gorgeous sight of the green tree. It was covered with hanging sparkles, and little toys, and charming frills, and it was lighted brightly with electric lights. The Yolka's branches were laden with glass cotton, light as puffs of snow, and on the tip of the tree was a brilliant star. Just as it should be!

"We have a Yolka!" Yefremov shrieked with delight.

"Yolka!" cried the sailors.

The tree was so beautiful, so bright, so real that it seemed a miracle. The sailors danced vigorously around it, singing their song of the Yolka that grew in the deep, green forests of Russia:

What merriment, what merriment,
We're here in happy throng.
We greet you, Yolka, gleefully
With season's gayest song.

Pavel, the cook, stood by the table with a proud grin, noticing how everyone sniffed and looked expectantly. Badigin had written in his latest article that the cook had worked several days on the preparation of the holiday supper. And what a supper it was! There were plenty of meat and fish dishes, and a platter of baked goodies was placed attractively in the middle of the table. The ship's dogs, Jerry and Icicle, sniffed excitedly all during the meal. The dogs had always had enough to eat, but on that New Year's Eve they were simply stuffed.

After supper, the dogs relaxed in the warm wardroom and sprawled under the table and dozed peacefully. Suddenly both of them jumped, bristled up, and barking loudly, dashed toward the door. Everyone in the cabin looked instantly toward the door . . . And there, smiling most genially, was Grandpa Frost himself. He walked slowly into the cabin, swinging heavily from side to side. He had a jolly red nose, and a long white beard. He was dressed properly in a long fur coat, and a big fat bag was slung across his shoulders. A real, honest to goodness Grandpa Frost such as can be seen in the pictures.

"Look at that!" cried Yefremov, pointing his finger at the large bag.

Grandpa Frost walked over calmly to the little Yolka and said, in a peculiarly familiar voice:

"Please, gentlemen, accept my gifts." He bowed ceremoniously and dug into his bag. Out came, first of all, an enormous pencil, the size of a flute. "This is for you, Konstantin Badigin, so that you can write *longer* articles for the papers." There was unmistakable sarcasm in the word longer, and everyone laughed.

Other presents followed. Yefremov, to his great delight, received the biggest package of all. When he untied the ribbon and unwrapped the newspaper, he found a box. Inside the box was another package wrapped in newspaper and tied with ribbon. When he untied and unwrapped that, he found another box. Everyone crowded around to see what was in *that* box. There was a third smaller package, and inside that a third, smaller box. Then came a fourth and a fifth box! Everyone roared with laughter as Yefremov continued unwrapping one box after another, each one smaller than the one before, of course. Finally, in the tenth box, there was the present. It was a very tiny baby doll. Yefremov held it in his big strong hands, and passed it around to all of his laughing comrades.

Pavel, the cook, received half a dozen pairs of dark glasses which protect the eyes from the blinding sparkle of snow when the sun shines. They were, of course, useless in the Arctic winter when there was no sun at all!

Fourteen times Grandpa Frost dipped his hand into the bag full of presents. When he put his hand in for the fifteenth time, he announced curiously, "And this is for me!" There was nothing there! Then he pulled off his beard, took off his fur coat, yanked off his red nose that had been pasted onto his face and became transformed into the radio engineer Nikolai Bekasov.

"So you are Grandpa Frost! Bekasov, you rascal!" shouted Badigin. They shook hands vigorously, in true Russian fashion, and Badigin bumped into the Yolka. As he touched the tree, somehow it didn't feel like a fir tree. "Look, comrades!" he shouted, inspecting the tree. "Look where our Yolka came from!" Everybody looked and touched the little green Yolka and gasped and laughed merrily at the discovery. For the beautiful Yolka proved to be homemade, not forest grown.

Nikolai Bekasov, with the help of several sailors, had thought up the trick of taking a stick and attaching to it twigs from the deck broom. This make-believe tree was colored and covered and became the homemade Yolka, perfectly fitting for the New Year's celebration in the Arctic.

To this day, the homemade broom-twig Yolka is in the Leningrad Arctic Museum, and all the men who had enjoyed it aboard ship are celebrating the season with a beautiful Yolka, a lovely green fir tree from the deep forests of Russia.

THE KISSING BUNCH STILL HANGS HIGH

Katherine VanEtten Lyford

WHILE Santa Claus plans his traditional roof-top-and chimney tour, training Donner and Blitzen to hedge-hop new television aerials, an older and more glamorous Christmas custom is being revived and adapted to modern homes. It's up again with the old kissing bunch, a sphere of spicy evergreens and mistletoe, the center of holiday festivities in Merrie England long before the Christmas tree was known.

A wonderful contraption, that Christmas kissing bunch! Beneath it Elizabethan boy met girl with explosive results, for custom demanded that "When a Man catch his Woman he may Kiss her until her Ears crack or she will be disappointed, if she is a Woman of any Spirit."

The making of the kissing bunch (sometimes called a kissing bough or ball) was traditionally a family affair and took place early on Christmas eve, as it was considered unlucky to bring holly into the house before that time. Cottages and castles were full of visiting cousins who helped to carry in the pile of fragrant greens, heaping them on the sanded floor in front of the open hearth. Three big barrel hoops were slipped one inside the other, tied at intersections with willow withes, and a fourth hoop slipped over the others to form a horizontal base for the candles. Then the winding of the hoops began, young and old good-naturedly disputing the merits of boxwood over yew, rosemary versus pine and ivy, and whether they would be prettier if dipped in water and sprinkled with flour to resemble snow.

Bachelor uncles tried to hide the rounded leaves of She-holly, bespeaking feminine control, and use only He-holly that guaranteed the man of the house would rule during the coming year. When caught at this, a lively scuffle ensued which was settled with forfeits to be redeemed beneath the kissing bunch.

Once the hoops were covered with greens, they were studded with rosettes of red and blue paper or bits of tin or mirrors. Candles were fastened to the horizontal hoop, and apples and oranges hung inside the bunch by bright satin streamers. Nativity figures were sometimes placed on a platform laid across the bottom intersections, so that the Holy Family was enclosed in a sphere of spicy greens. Just beneath them a big bunch of mistletoe was tied, and the kissing bunch was ready to be hung.

The trimmers gathered around to watch, as the big ball was suspended from its own special hook, far enough away from the hearth to escape a flying spark, but not too near any shadowy corner in which grey-bearded Sylvester, the Spirit of the Old Year, might be lurking, ready to dash out and snatch a kiss from an unwary girl. Once the candles were lighted, grandfather put by his churchwarden's pipe and came forward to claim the Christmas privilege of soundly bussing each feminine guest. After that, it was "kiss as catch can" throughout the holidays.

If a careful scrutiny revealed no squinting, flat-footed woman or barefooted man (either would ruin Yule magic), a huge log was hauled in and placed beneath the kissing bunch. Here it immediately became Don the Carthorse, stuck in the mud. Teams of guests were chosen to pull him out, with long ropes slipped about the rough bark. Yanking first this way, then that, each team tried to roll Don to the hearth while keeping their rivals from doing the same thing.

If thou art Don, we'll draw three from
  the mire
Of this (save reverence) love, wherein
  thou stick'st up to the ears,

they shouted, as the tug of war went on with frequent interruptions to kiss any player caught beneath the kissing bunch. On reaching the hearth, Don became the Yule Log, seat of honor for the youngest guest who sang a Christmas song, and was rewarded with Yule "bawbie" (taffy).

Then followed a round of games—blind man's buff, a yawning match with cheese for a prize, puss in the corner, turn the trencher, and jumping for cakes dipped in treacle—all ages joining in, happy to be children once more. A knock at the door and in rushed the Goosey Dancers, a group of masqueraders, who lined up under the kissing bunch to act out in pantomime the age-old legend of Saint George, the Dragon, the Father Christmas. Ending this impromptu drama, the actors raised their young voices in the traditional Goosey Dancers' song, while a raggle-taggle Betsey Beelzebub passed round the hat—

> We are not daily beggars,
> That beg from door to door
> But we are neighbors' children
> Who you have seen before.
> Bring us out a table
> And set it with a cloth,
> Bring us out a mouldy cheese
> And some of your Christmas loaf.

After they had been fed, the Goosey Dancers stayed to spoon the posset. This was a fine, fast, unhygienic game, for which each one brought his own spoon. On a table beneath the kissing bunch was set a great deep bowl filled to the brim with posset, a foaming mixture of ale, milk, and nutmeg. Hidden in the depths were thimble, ring, and coin. At a given signal, everyone began to spoon the posset from bowl to mouth, hoping each time to dip up one of the omens of fortune. How they cheered when the ragged shepherd got the coin, grandfather won the thimble, and the five-year-old daughter of the piper spooned up the ring!

Until Twelfth Night, when it was dismantled and hoops and trimmings stored away for next year, the kissing bunch continued to be the center of Christmas fun. Standing beneath it, the head couple led off the quadrille as the piper's bagpipes skirled "Speed the Plough" or "Bernie Bough." In its fragrant candlelight, grandmother gathered the youngest grandchildren to tell them the story of the first

Christmas. Under it the family ate its Christmas dinner of boar's head, roast goose, Sir Loyne of Beef, plumb pudding, and Christmas pye. Afterward, those who were still able to move, played snapdragon, snatching raisins from the burning brandy. Then came the climax of Christmas day, the harvesting of the fruit of the kissing bunch, small brightly wrapped gifts that had appeared by magic overnight to hang enticingly over the heads of excited, impatient children.

THE CHRISTMAS TREE SHIP
Harry Hansen

CHRISTMAS in Chicago, fifty years ago, was a happy, home festival in a city not yet too rich, too pretentious, to be neighborly. There was usually snow at Christmas; it lay in large heaps in the gutters and was packed solid on the streets. When snow fell it was heavy with moisture; it blocked trains and held up streetcars. The average citizen shoveled his own sidewalks clean and looked after his own fires. A few blocks beyond the Loop, where the gray wooden cottages with their scrollwork porches stretched for miles, householders would be out early in the mornings wielding their shovels, amid shouts to their neighbors, for in those days families lived long enough in one locality to become known to one another.

In the houses on the near North Side, where brick buildings abounded, the windows had little wooden blinds inside through which came the yellow rays of light from gas jets. The air in the streets outside had the close feeling of a low-ceilinged room and shouts rebounded from wall to wall. In that air, bells on sleighs jingled in time a long way off and hoofbeats made a dull patter on the packed snow. As the sleigh passed under the light of the gas lamp at the corner you could see the prancing horse, the curved dashboard, the gleam of the nickeled bars across the front, the flash of the runners. The driver would be wearing a wide fur

collar and a fur cap; the woman beside him would be tucked under fur robes and look very comfortable in a brown fur neckpiece and toque.

Inside, the house was warm and a bit stuffy with dry air. The carpets had a firm surface and gay curlicues of vine leaves all over them. The hall might be dark; its walls were covered with embossed paper, stained to the color of leather, and the gaslight flickered behind a globe of pink glass ornamented with a trailing vine. You walked quickly past the parlor, which had a mantelpiece of black slate and a mirror over the fireplace and heavy chairs and settees with curved walnut legs, to the back room where all the family gathered. Here the walls were hung with photographs of young and old, and there were music racks and bookshelves. If the house was heated by a furnace, the hot air flooded up through a register in the floor, but more likely a big-bellied stove, consuming anthracite coal, gleamed red through mica windows in a corner. And in the bay stood the Christmas tree.

Most likely the father of the family had picked it out and carried it home. Men and women carried their own bundles in those days. Perhaps he walked down to the Clark Street bridge, a week or two before Christmas, to see if the Schuenemanns had come down from Wisconsin with a load of spruce trees. Invariably the two big, brawny lads would be there with a fishing schooner loaded with trees that they themselves had cut in the Michigan woods. They were fine, well-shaped trees and cost so little—for 75 cents you bought a full-sized tree; for a dollar you had your choice of the best. Even saplings provided bright decorations for a city where people were making money, but not too much money, and where the average citizen was always fearful of hard times.

As long ago as 1887, the two Schuenemanns, Herman and August, had sailed down in a schooner from Manistique, Michigan, with a load of spruce and tied up beside the dock behind the old red brick commission houses at the Clark Street bridge. There, Chicago found them and bought their stock, and called Herman captain, and remembered to look for him the following year. When snow fell on Chicago's streets in December days, the father of the family would say, "Guess I'll have to go down to the Clark Street bridge to see if the captain is in and get us a tree."

Fifty years ago the work of providing trees for Christmas was not yet the mass-production business it has become in recent times. No dealer contracted for thousands of trees as a speculation and destroyed great numbers if he had guessed wrong on the demand. No man cut down whole hillsides to satisfy the whims of people who followed a custom but didn't know how to pray. There were plenty of trees for all. The Schuenemanns went into the woods behind Manistique and Thompson, Michigan, where young trees grew on land that had been cut over to make the lumber that went into mid-western houses a generation before. They chose the trees carefully, including some tall ones for which they had orders from churches and hotels. Sometimes they had to work in the snow, and when the trees reached Chicago there was still snow on the branches. The brothers thought they had done well when they made a modest profit on a trip that occupied about six weeks of the wintry

season, when it was hard to haul other cargoes.

The work was not easy, neither the cutting nor the sailing, for they always came when Lake Michigan kicked up a lot of rough sea. In 1898, August had just set sail with a load of trees when a storm arose and he and his ship were lost. Thereupon Herman determined to carry on alone. In 1899 he was back at the Clark Street dock with his boat, the *Rouse Simmons,* loaded with Christmas trees. He was a jovial man, with a very ruddy complexion and laughing wrinkles around his blue eyes, and everybody liked him.

For eleven years Herman arrived with his cargo, and many people depended on him for a tree year after year. Then came the hard season of 1912, with storms and heavy seas on Lake Michigan. Late in November, Herman cut his trees in the woods behind Manistique and started for Chicago in the *Rouse Simmons,* with a crew of seventeen men. There were head winds and heavy seas from the start, and soon the schooner was struggling in a raging snowstorm. What took place on board we can only guess. The *Rouse Simmons* sailed into the silence that covers all the fine ships that have fallen victim to the gales of Lake Michigan, which have taken the lives of so many.

Long before Chicago missed the *Rouse Simmons* at its dock, reports began to come in of the ship's distress. A schooner resembling it was said to have been sighted off Kewaunee, Wisconsin, flying distress signals. The steamer *George W. Orr* reported to the revenue cutter *Tuscarora* that she had seen the *Rouse Simmons* three miles offshore, but the captain later admitted that he might have been mistaken. But on December 5, 1912, fishermen off Two Rivers Point, seven miles north of Manitowoc, Wisconsin, found the tops of spruce trees entangled in their nets. Trees had been roped together on the deck of the *Rouse Simmons,* and how could they get into the lake at that point if not off a ship?

On December 13, a watcher on the beach at Sheboygan, Wisconsin, reported that he had picked up a bottle containing a message that came from the captain. It had been written on a page of the ship's log and read:

"Friday — Everybody goodbye. I guess we are all through. Sea washed over our deckload Thursday. During the night the small boat was washed over. Leaking bad. Ingvald and Steve fell overboard Thursday. God help us.

Herman Schuenemann"

The men referred to were believed to have been Steve E. Nelson, mate, and Ingvald Nylons, seaman. But if there was such a message, it never reached the captain's wife, who was eagerly waiting for scraps of news in her Manistique home. She was a valiant little woman, with a great deal of stamina. When she realized that her three little girls, Elsie and the twins, Pearl and Hazel, were now dependent wholly on her efforts, she resolved to take up her husband's task.

There was no Christmas ship at the Clark Street dock in 1912. But when 1913 came, Chicago residents who looked over the railings of the bridge beheld another schooner, loaded with trees, as in the days when Captain Herman held forth there. On board was the plucky little wife of the captain. She had gone into the woods with the woodcutters and supervised the felling of the trees. With her, too, were her girls, as well as women to weave wreaths and garlands. Chicago was to become well acquainted with the Schuenemanns. They were to come season after season for 22 years after the *Rouse Simmons* went down.

For years Chicago friends would ask the captain's wife whether there had been any definite report on the *Rouse Simmons,* and she could only shake her head sorrowfully. Yet the sea, which guards its secrets well, reluctantly gave up tangible evidence 14 years after the disaster. On April 23, 1924, the wallet of Captain Schuenemann was found at Two Rivers Point, where the spruce trees had been tangled in the fishermen's nets. It still had the original rubber band around it and the cards and clippings inside seemed to be made of plaster. Some of the clippings related to earlier voyages of the Christmas tree ship. Three years after this find, a bottle with a note signed by Charles Nelson was picked up. It read:

"These lines were written at 10:30 P.M. Schooner R. S. ready to go down about 20 miles southeast Two Rivers Point between fifteen or twenty miles off shore. All hands lashed to one line. Goodbye."

Eventually the family made its last voyage to the Chicago market with Christmas trees. The mother had grown gray; the girls were handsome young women. Forty-seven years had elapsed since Herman, as an 18-year-old lad, had steered his first cargo into Chicago. The ship had become an institution.

Its fame grew. Today, when the winds blow hard on the lake and the heavy surf pounds the frozen shore line, watchers in the lighthouse recall the *Rouse Simmons.* Long ago it inspired a ballad. When word of its loss reached Chicago newspapers, Vincent Starrett, bibliophile and author of many books of fiction and belles-lettres, was a reporter on the *Daily News.* His editor was Henry Justin Smith. "It would make a fine ballad," said Starrett. "Why don't you write it?" replied Smith. So Starrett composed "The Ballad of the Christmas Ship," a poem of many, many quatrains, and Smith found room for it among the crowded columns of the day's news. It may never challenge the efforts of youthful orators as often as "The Wreck of the Hesperus," but the legend is just as moving and the intentions of the poet were as good as Longfellow's.

Children's Books About the Christmas Tree

A SELECTED LIST of Christmas tree stories, plays, poems, and carols for the pleasure of children and all who are young at heart.

By PRISCILLA SAWYER LORD

ALDEN, RAYMOND L., *Christmas Tree Land*. New York: Bobbs-Merrill, 1912

BISHOP, CLAIRE HUCHET, *Happy Christmas*. New York: Daye, 1956

BROCK, EMMA L., *The Birds' Christmas Tree*. New York: Knopf, 1946

BROWN, MARGARET WISE, *The Little Fir Tree*. New York: Thomas Y. Crowell, 1954

BUCK, PEARL S., *Christmas Miniature*. New York: John Day, 1956

CHENEY, CORA, *The Christmas Tree Hessian*. New York: Henry Holt, 1957

CROWLEY, MAUDE, *Azor and the Blue-eyed Cow*. New York: Oxford, 1951

DURYEA, ELIZABETH, *The Long Christmas Eve*. Boston: Houghton Mifflin, 1954

EATON, ANNE THAXTER, *The Animals' Christmas*. New York: Viking, 1944

ENRIGHT, ELIZABETH, *A Christmas Tree for Lydia*. New York: Rinehart, 1947

FOX, FRANCES MARGARET, *Legends of the Christ Child*. New York: Sheed and Ward, 1941

GORDON, PATRICIA, *The Heir to Christmas*. New York: Viking, 1955

GOUDGE, ELIZABETH, *The Sister of the Angels*. New York: Coward McCann, 1939

HULL, HELEN SCHUYLER, *The Gift*. New York: Macmillan, 1957

KELLY, ERIC P., *The Christmas Nightingale; three Christmas Stories from Poland*. New York: Macmillan, 1932

KINGMAN, LEE, *The Magic Christmas Tree*. New York: Ariel Books, Farrar, Strauss, Cudahy, 1956

LITERATURE COMMITTEE OF THE ASSOCIATION FOR CHILDHOOD EDUCATION, *Told Under the Christmas Tree; an Umbrella Book*. New York: Macmillan, 1948

LOVELACE, MAUD HART, *The Trees Kneel at Christmas*. New York: Thomas Y. Crowell, 1951

MILHOUS, KATHERINE, *Snow Over Bethlehem*. New York: Scribners, 1945

MILHOUS, KATHERINE, *With Bells On*. New York: Scribners, 1955

OLDS, HELEN DIEHL, *Christmas-Tree Sam*. New York: Julian Messner, 1952

PAULI, HERTHA, *The Story of the Christmas Tree*. Boston: Houghton Mifflin, 1944

PEARY, MARIE AHNIGHITO, *Little Tooktoo: Story of Santa Claus' Youngest Reindeer*. New York: William Morrow, 1930.

PRITCHARD, VIRGINIA COLE, *A Christmas Story*. New York: E. P. Dutton, 1939

SAWYER, RUTH, *The Long Christmas*. New York: Viking, 1946

SEYMOUR, ALTA HALVERSON, *A Grandma for Christmas*. Philadelphia: The Westminster Press, 1946

SMITH, ELVA SOPHRONIA AND HAZELTINE, ALICE ISABEL, *The Christmas Book of Legends and Stories*. New York: Lothrop, Lee & Shepard, 1944

SMITH, SUSAN, *The Christmas Tree in the Woods*. New York: Minton, Balch, 1932

THOMPSON, DOROTHY, *Once on Christmas*. New York: Oxford, 1938

TUDOR, TASHA, *The Dolls' Christmas*. New York: Oxford, 1950

TURNER, THYRA, *Christmas House: The Story of a Visit from St. Nicholas*. New York: Scribners, 1943

VANCE, MARGUERITE, *A Star for Hansi*. New York: Harper, 1936

WALLOWER, LUCILLE, *The Morning Star*. New York: David McKay, 1957

WRIGHT, KATHERINE O., *Christmas at Thunder Gap*. New York: Arrowhead Books, 1954

YATES, ELIZABETH, *Once in the Year*. New York: Coward-McCann, 1947

SPECIAL STORIES

EGGLESTON, MARGARET W., The Christmas Angel in *Thirty Stories I Like to Tell* by Margaret Eggleston. New York: Harper, 1949

GOUDGE, ELIZABETH, The Legend of the First Christmas Tree in *The Reward of Faith* by Elizabeth Goudge. New York: Coward-McCann, 1950

GRAY, ELIZABETH JANET, Christmas Cherries in *Feasts and Frolics* by Phyllis R. Fenner. New York: Knopf, 1949

HALE, LUCRETIA P., The Peterkins' Christmas Tree in *Told Under the Christmas Tree* compiled by Frances Cavanah. New York: Grosset and Dunlap, 1941

HARDY, ROSE L., The Animals' Christmas Tree in *A Holiday Story Sampler* by Charlotte Conover. Chicago: Albert Whitman, 1941

LILLIE, AMY MORRIS, The Fir on Oak Ridge in *The Book of Three Festivals* by Amy Morris Lillie. New York: E. P. Dutton, 1948

LOHSE, CHARLOTTE, Christmas in Summer in *Feasts and Frolics* selected by Phyllis R. Fenner. New York: Alfred A. Knopf, 1949

SHIPPEN, KATHERINE B., The Christmas Tree in *Santa's Footprints and Other Christmas Stories*. New York: Aladdin Books, 1948

PLAYS

ALLAN, DOROTHY C., *Christmas Trees for Sale:* a play in one act. Boston: Walter H. Baker, 1941

CAPELL, LORETTA CAMP, The First Christmas Tree in *A Treasury of Christmas Plays* edited by Sylvia E. Kamerman. Boston: Plays, Inc., 1958

DUVALL, LUCILLE M., Little Chip's Christmas Tree in *A Treasury of Christmas Plays* edited by Sylvia E. Kamerman. Boston: Plays, Inc., 1958

FAWCETT, MARGARET GEORGIA, The Talking Christmas Tree in *A Treasury of Christmas Plays* edited by Sylvia E. Kamerman. Boston: Plays, Inc., 1958

MARTENS, ANNE COULTER, *The Tiniest Christmas Tree*. Boston: Walter H. Baker, 1956

WILDE, PERCIVAL, *The Enchanted Christmas Tree*. Boston: Walter H. Baker, 1946

WILSON, DOROTHY CLARKE, *And Myrrh*. Boston: Walter H. Baker, 1935

POETRY AND CAROLS

BREWTON, SARA AND JOHN E., *Christmas Bells Are Ringing*. New York: Macmillan, 1951

FARJEON, ELEANOR, *Eleanor Farjeon's Poems for Children*. New York: Lippincott, 1926

JOHNSON, EMILIE FENDALL, *A Little Book of Prayers*. New York: Viking Press, 1941

KARASZ, ILONKA, *The Twelve Days of Christmas*. New York: Harper, 1949

LANGSTAFF, JOHN, *On Christmas Day in the Morning*. New York: Harcourt, Brace, 1959

REY, H. A., *We Three Kings and Other Christmas Carols*. New York: Harper, 1944

SHAHN, BEN, *A Partridge in a Pear Tree*. The Museum of Modern Art, New York: Doubleday, 1949

ESPECIALLY FOR ADULTS

CARROLL, GLADYS HASTY, *While the Angels Sing*. New York: Macmillan, 1947

CHASE, MARY ELLEN, *Recipe For a Magic Childhood*. New York: Macmillan, 1952

LOHAN, ROBERT, *Christmas Tales for Reading Aloud*. New York: Daye, 1946

VIGUERS, RUTH HILL, Open the Windows and Let Christmas In! (reprint from *The Horn Book Magazine*). Boston: The Horn Book, 1954

WAGENKNECHT, EDWARD, *The Fireside Book of Christmas Stories*. New York: Bobbs-Merrill, 1943

Bibliography

No ATTEMPT has been made to list such references as the Old Testament, the New Testament, the Apocryphal Scriptures, and various encyclopedias consulted. Also countless issues of English and American periodicals (published from 1840 to 1959), in addition to newspaper articles, brochures, pamphlets, and other materials in the author's files have provided background material.

Access to the extensive private library of Christmas literature owned by Priscilla Sawyer Lord has made the task of research both pleasant and profitable.

HOW-TO-DO-IT-BOOKS

BAER, BARBARA, *Christmas Make-it Book*. New York: Hearthside, 1954. A handy book full of pictures, sketches and ideas for easy and effective decorations.

CHANEY, ELSA, *The Twelve Days of Christmas*. Collegeville, Minnesota: The Liturgical Press, 1955. The religious symbolism of Christmas and how it can be observed by the family. Excellent for Christmas aspects of the liturgy.

CHRISMAN, IRMA, *Christmas Trees, Decorations and Ornaments*. New York: Hearthside, 1956. Wide selection of ideas, photographs, and drawings.

GANNON, RUTH, *New Ways with Dried Arrangements*. New York: Studio Publications, Viking Press, 1958. Comprehensive coverage on drying and using plant material for decoration.

GRAILVILLE WRITING CENTER, *The Twelve Days of Christmas Kit*. Collegeville, Minnesota: The Liturgical Press, 1955. Stresses the liturgical aspect of Christmas decoration with complete set of cardboard cutouts ready to use.

LAGORCE, LOUISE, *The Christmas Cookie Tree*. Boston: Chapman & Grimes, 1959. Contains recipes, procedure, patterns.

LISTAITE, M. GRATIA (SISTER) AND HILDEBRAND, NORBERT A., *A New Look at Christmas Decorations*. Milwaukee: Bruce, 1957. Most complete book of it kind on decorations inspired by various countries. How-to-do-it techniques.

ROBERTS, PATRICIA EASTERBROOK, *Decorations for Christmas and Other Occasions*. New York: Studio Publications, Crowell, 1954. Illustrated, with ideas and suggestions for entertaining.

SAROS, THEODORE A., *Christmas Lighting and Decorating*. New York: Van Nostrand, 1954. Covers the subject from every angle and offers sound techniques for safety. Well illustrated.

SCHULKE, ZELDA WYATT, *A Treasury of Christmas Decorations*. New York: Hearthside, 1957. Many original ideas by a competent and skilled flower arranger with excellent photographs.

VAN RENSSELAER, ELEANOR, *Decorating with Pods and Cones*. Princeton, N. J.: Van Nostrand, 1957. Describes how to make all kinds of decorations and trees from cones and pods.

WAUGH, DOROTHY, *A Handbook of Christmas Decoration*. New York: Macmillan, 1958. How-to-do-it told and illustrated with more than 350 sketches and photographs.

WERTSNER, ANNE, *Make Your Own Merry Christmas*. New York: Barrows, 1946. A long-time favorite written for a wide audience. Well illustrated.

WHITE, GWEN, *A World of Pattern*. Boston: C. T. Branford, 1958. A fascinating book full of designs.

ADDISON, JAMES THAYER, *The Episcopal Church in the United States*. New York: Scribner, 1951

AULD, WILLIAM MUIR, *Christmas Traditions*. New York: Macmillan, 1931

BARNETT, JAMES H., *The American Christmas*. New York: Macmillan, 1954

BARNUM, P. T., *The Life of P. T. Barnum*. New York: Redfield, 1855

BEERBOHM, MAX, *A Christmas Garland*. New York: Dutton, 1912

BENSON, E. F., *As We Were*. New York: Longmans, Green, 1930

BISHOP, JOSEPH BUCKLIN, *Theodore Roosevelt's Letters to His Children*. New York: Scribner, 1919

BOWDITCH, H. I. (DR.), *Christmas Tree of the Bowditch Family*. Privately Printed, 1886

BRACE, CHARLES LORING, *Home-Life in Germany*. New York: Scribner, 1853

BRAND, JOHN, *Observations on Popular Antiquities*. London: Chatto & Windus, 1888

BUDAY, GEORGE, *The History of the Christmas Card*. London: Rockliff, 1954

BUTTERWORTH, HEZEKIAH, *Christmas in America*. Boston: Dana Estes, 1894

CAGNER, EWERT, *Swedish Christmas*. Sweden: Tre Trychare, 1955

CATTON, BRUCE, *American Heritage, Vol. 8, No. 1*. New York: American Heritage Publishing Co., 1956

CHAMBERS, E. K., *The Medieval Stage*, 2 vols. London: Oxford, 1925

CHAMBERS, ROBERT, Ed., *Book of Days*, 2 vols. Philadelphia, Lippincott, 1914

CHAPMAN, ARTHUR G. AND WRAY, ROBERT D., *Christmas Trees for Pleasure and Profit*. New Brunswick, N. J.. Rutgers University Press, 1957

COLLIS, JOHN STEWART, *The Triumph of the Tree*. New York: Sloane, 1954

COMMAGER, HENRY STEELE, *The St. Nicholas Anthology*. New York: Random House, 1948

COURT, EARL W., *4000 Years of Christmas*. New York: Schuman, 1948

CRIPPEN, T. G., *Christmas and Christmas Lore*. London: Blackie, 1923

DEARMER, PERCY, *The Oxford Book of Carols*. London: Oxford, 1928

DEROBECK, NESTA, *The Christmas Crib*. Milwaukee: Bruce, 1934

DEROBECK, NESTA, *St. Francis, the Herald of the Great King*, Assisi, 1950

DICKENS, CHARLES, *Christmas Stories*. Boston: Estes & Lauriat, 1882

DYER, T. F. THISELTON, *The Folk-Lore of Plants*. New York: Appleton, 1889

FOLEY, DANIEL J., *Little Saints of Christmas*. Boston: Dresser, Chapman Grimes, 1959

FOLKARD, RICHARD, *Plant Lore, Legends, and Lyrics*. London: Sampson, Low, Marston, 1892

FOLLEN, CHARLES, *The Works of Charles Follen*. Boston: Hilliard, Gray, 1842

FORD, LAUREN, *The Ageless Story*. New York: Dodd, Mead & Co., 1939

FRAZER, J. G., *The Golden Bough*. New York: Macmillan, 1923

FREEMAN, MARGARET, *The Story of the Three Kings*. New York: Metropolitan Museum of Art, 1955

FREEMAN, RUTH AND LARRY, *Cavalcade of Toys*. New York: Century House, 1942

FRENCH, W. H. AND HALE, C. B., *Middle English Metrical Romances*. New York: Prentice-Hall, 1940

GARDNER, HORACE J., *Let's Celebrate Christmas*. New York: Barnes, 1940

GORELY, JEAN, *Queen Charlotte's Christmas Tree*. Boston: Privately printed, 1945

GOUDGE, ELIZABETH, *The White Witch*. New York: Coward-McCann, 1958

GREEN, SAMUEL G. (REV.), *French Pictures*. London: The Religious Tract Society, 1878

GRIGSON, GEOFFREY, *The Englishman's Flora*. London: Phoenix House, 1955

HALE, E. E. (REV.) AND SUSAN A., *A Family Flight*. Boston: Lothrop, 1881

HALE, EDWARD E., *Christmas Eve and Christmas Day*. Boston: Roberts Brothers, 1873

HAMPDEN, JOHN, *Sir William and the Wolf*. New York: E. P. Dutton, 1960

HARRISON, MICHAEL, *The Story of Christmas*. London: Odhams Press

HAUGAN, RALPH E., *Christmas, an American Annual of Christmas Literature and Art*. Vols. 1-29. Minneapolis: Augsburg Publishing House, 1959

HERVEY, THOMAS K., *The Book of Christmas*. New York: Wiley & Putnam, 1845

HOLLAND, HENRY SCOTT AND ROCKSTRO, W. S., *Memoir of Madame Jenny Lind-Goldschmidt*. New York: Scribner, 1891. Vols. 1 & 2

HORN, ALOYSIUS, *A Christmas Chronicle*. Paterson, N. J.: St. Anthony's Guild Press, 1941

HOTTES, ALFRED CARL, 1001 *Christmas Facts and Fancies*. New York: De la Mare, 1937

HOWARD, BLANCHE, *One Year Abroad*. Boston: Osgood, 1877

HUTH, OTTO, *Der Lichterbaum*. Berlin: 1943

HUTTON, ANN HAWKES, *Portrait of Patriotism*. Philadelphia: Chilton, 1959

JACKSON, F. NEVILL (MRS.), *Toys of Other Days*. New York: Scribner, 1908

JOHNSON, ANNA C., *Peasant Life in Germany*. New York: Scribner, 1858

KANE, HARNETT T., *The Southern Christmas Book*. New York: McKay, 1958

KARASZ, ILONKA, *The Twelve Days of Christmas*. New York: Harper, 1949

KELLEHER, D. L., *An Anthology of Christmas Prose and Verse,* London: Cresset Press, 1928

KRYTHE, MAYMIE R., *All About Christmas*. New York: Harper, 1954

LA GORCE, LOUISE, *The Christmas Cookie Tree*. Boston: Chapman & Grimes, 1959

LEWIS, D. B. WYNDHAM AND HASELTINE, G. C., *A Christmas Book*. New York: Dutton, 1928

LOWELL, EDWARD J., *The Hessians in the Revolution*. New York: Harper, 1884

MABIE, HAMILTON W., *Book of Christmas*. New York: Macmillan, 1909

McKNIGHT, GEORGE H., *St. Nicholas*. New York: Putnam, 1917

MANROSS, WILLIAM WILSON, *A History of the American Episcopal Church*. Milwaukee: Morehouse, 1935

MILES, CLEMENT A., *Christmas in Ritual and Tradition, Christian and Pagan*. London: Unwin, 1912

MONKS, JAMES L., *Great Catholic Festivals*. New York: Schuman, 1951

MULLINS, RUTH E., *Religious Themes in Flower Arrangement*. New York: Hearthside Press, 1959

MURPHY, WILLIAM H., *Kriss Kringle's Raree Show for Good Boys and Girls*. New York: Murphy, 1847

RAHNER, HUGO, *Griechische Mythen in Christlicher Deutung*. Zurich: Rhein-Verlag, 1945

RICHARDS, KATHERINE L., *How Christmas Came to the Sunday Schools*. New York: Dodd, Mead & Co., 1934

ROEHRENBECK, WILLIAM J., *Christmastide*. New York: Stephen Daye, 1948

ROSENBERG, C. G., *Jenny Lind in America*. New York: Stringer & Townsend, 1851

SHOEMAKER, ALFRED L., *Christmas in Pennsylvania*. Kutztown, Pennsylvania: Pennsylvania Folklife Society, 1959

SIDGWICK, ALFRED (MRS.), *Home Life in Germany*. New York: Macmillan, 1908

SOWDER, ARTHUR M., *Christmas Trees—the Tradition and Trade*. Bulletin No. 24, U.S.D.A., Washington, D. C., 1957

SPAMER, ADOLF, *Weihnachten in alter und neuer Zeit*. G. Jena, 1937

THEN, J. N., *Christmas Comes Again*. Milwaukee: Bruce, 1940

TILLE, ALEXANDER, *Yule and Christmas*. London: David Nutt, 1899

UNITED STATES DEPARTMENT OF AGRICULTURE, *Trees—The Yearbook of Agriculture, 1949*. Washington, D. C.: Government Printing Office, 1949

VAN DYKE, HENRY, *The First Christmas Tree*. New York: Scribner, 1897

VANN, GERALD, *The Paradise Tree*. New York: Sheed & Ward, 1959

VLOBERG, MAURICE, *Les Noëls de France*. Paris: B. Arthaud, 1953

WAGENKNECHT, EDWARD, *A Fireside Book of Yuletide Tales*. New York: Bobbs-Merrill, 1948

WALSH, WILLIAM S., *Curiosities of Popular Customs*. Phila: Lippincott, 1898

WEISER, FRANCIS X., *Handbook of Christian Feasts and Customs*. New York: Harcourt, Brace, 1952

WEISER, FRANCIS X., *Religious Customs in the Family*. Collegeville, Minnesota: The Liturgical Press, 1956

WEISER, FRANCIS X., *The Christmas Book*. New York: Harcourt, Brace, 1952

WERNECKE, HERBERT H., *Christmas Customs Around the World*. Philadelphia: Westminster Press, 1959

YOUNG, K., *The Drama of the Medieval Church,* 2 Vols. London: Oxford, 1933

Index